CALLING ALL AUTHORS

How to Publish with Your Eyes Wide Open

Revealing Publishing Myths, Misconceptions and Realities for Published Authors & Writers Who Dream of Becoming Authors

Includes Conversations and Commentaries
from the popular internet program
CALLING ALL AUTHORS

VALERIE CONNELLY

© 2007
Nightengale Press
A Nightengale Media LLC Company

CALLING ALL AUTHORS

Copyright ©2007 by Valerie Connelly
Cover Design ©2007 by Nightengale Press

All rights reserved. Printed in the United States of America. No part of this book may be reproduced or transmitted in any form or by any means, electronic or mechanical, including photocopying, recording, or by any information storage and retrieval system without written permission from the publisher, except for the inclusion of brief quotations in articles and reviews. If you purchased this book without a cover, you should be aware that this book is stolen property. It was reported as "unsold and destroyed" to the publisher, and neither the author nor the publisher has received any payment for this "stripped book."

For information about Nightengale Press please
visit our website at www.nightengalepress.com.
Email: publisher@nightengalepress.biz
or send a letter to:
Nightengale Press
10936 N. Port Washington Road. Suite 206
Mequon, WI 53092
Library of Congress Cataloging-in-Publication Data

Connelly, Valerie,
    Calling All Authors/ Valerie Connelly
    ISBN:1-933449-43-8
    Writing/Publishing/Marketing

Copyright Registered: 2007
First Published by Nightengale Press in the USA

August 2007

10 9 8 7 6 5 4 3 2 1

Printed in the United States

ENDORSEMENTS

Calling All Authors *may be the best information that's come out in years for aspiring new authors. It will definitely guide them through the many land mines that exist in today's complex publishing scene.*
— Patrika Vaughn, President, A Cappela Publishing

Calling All Authors *is a well-organized and much-needed guide.*
— Maryglenn McCombs, Maryglenn McCombs Book Publicity

Calling All Authors — *An excellent resource for new authors.*
— Eric Gruber, ArticleMarketingExperts.com

I think Calling All Authors *provides outstanding guidance to authors and should give them helpful information about issues that publishers, editors face and how an author can help simplify those issues. An excellent work!*
— Bob Gussin, Oceanview Publishing

Valerie Connelly is the author's advocate, and Calling All Authors *demonstrates her commitment to helping fellow authors fulfill their writing and publishing goals. Comprehensive and well-organized, this book covers all of the key elements associated with writing and publishing — and in so doing, it answers the common questions many writers have when considering the daunting task of publishing their work.* **Calling all Authors** *is an excellent source of information for published and unpublished writers alike.*

— Zara Griswold, author of Surrogacy Was the Way, and founder of **Family Source Consultants** Surrogacy and Egg Donation Agency. www.FamilySourceSurrogacy.com

Calling All Authors *is a clearly written, thorough primer for both new and less experienced authors to increase their chances of a successful book selling experience. Valerie Connelly has written a guide to educate authors as to the fine points of book publicity and book sales.*

—Barb Radmore, Editor, Front Street Reviews

Regardless of your publishing method, Calling All Authors *is a must-read for anyone attempting to publish a book. Vital "how-to" information to make the publishing journey easier and more successful!*

—Yvonne Perry, Author of Right to Recover: Winning the Political and Religious Wars over Stem Cell Research in America and Owner of **Write On! Creative Writing Services**

Valerie combines her vast experience as publisher, author, educator and talk show host with the best marketing strategies of her guests. Calling All Authors *presents a rich cornucopia of ideas on how to publish and prosper as authors - without the usual cookie-cutter advice.*
—Francine Silverman, author of Talk Radio for Authors

I wish I had paid more attention to Chapter 4 and the sound advice it gives. WRITE, EDIT, REWRITE AND RE-EDIT. No more positive advice can be given any writer, before the copy is sent off to print.
—Chuck McCann, Author of Short, Shorter and Shorter Stories and Osmis, the Cursed Egyptian Maiden

📖 DEDICATION

To all authors, published and unpublished, who look at the power of the written word and cannot resist partaking of the cup overflowing with this eternally optimistic hope: that, you, too, can express, share, inform, and entertain the reading population of the world and compete among the titans of the publishing world, all the while enjoying the rigors of the game.

INTRODUCTION

The waters are deep and swift in the publishing world. Many are swept away in the currents of trends, hype, broken promises and confusion. The options are many and the rewards can be great, but the road is much longer and the trials much more challenging than the writer who dreams of publishing a book can imagine. So many believe that the manuscript they have labored to write will be the next best-seller, yet they have no idea of how a best-seller is made. In fact, many do not even know what the term "best-seller" actually means beyond their ever so innocent impressions from reading blurbs on book jackets: "New York Times Best Selling Book."

This book, CALLING ALL AUTHORS, is meant to separate fact from fiction. It is not altogether a "how-to" book. It is a book about dispelling misconceptions and revealing realities in publishing. It is about the business of writing, publishing and marketing a salable book. The un-initiated, would-be author and those who have tried and failed to produce the mega-hit of the century, will learn from this book what they have done or can do correctly and what they should avoid doing at all costs. It is based on first-hand experience of my own, and much of the information presented is drawn from the experience of other experts in publishing, publicity, marketing and writing, all of whom have appeared in 2006 on CALLING ALL AUTHORS, the weekly radio program, which I host on Global Talk Radio.

I intend to provide insight and commentary that provokes the hopeful author to take a step back, look at what becoming successfully published really entails, and then provide that author with the tools to step into the fray with knowledge to compliment his courage and out-and-out foolhardiness. Yes, it takes an undying belief in your book, money, persistence, and the willingness to keep pressing forward when sales sag more than an octogenarian's jowls.

Publishing a book and seeing it through the dark times, when the euphoria of getting published in the first place has worn off, when your publisher has forgotten your name, and when you begin to wonder why you ever thought your book was worth all the expense and trouble it has caused you, is still the single most rewarding experience a literate human being can have. There is nothing more satisfying than holding your book in your hand for the first time, or seeing your book on the local bookstore's shelves, or available on Amazon.com, BarnesandNoble.com and on your own publisher's website for all to see and purchase. And, there is nothing more disappointing than not getting any sales, except perhaps showing up to sing for a nightclub gig and having no audience arrive to listen.

I hope all authors who read this book, already published authors or those who contemplate leaping into the ocean of more than 280,000 books per year that are published in the United States alone, will find the tools, the inspiration, the encouragement and the will to do what it takes to make their books into their own personal best-sellers. I hope you will be enlightened and empowered to follow your dream and your gut instincts about your work as an author, and that you will find good advice and some help among these pages.

—Valerie Connelly
Author, Publisher, Talk Show Host and Speaker

ACKNOWLEDGEMENTS

All the many expert and author guests on CALLING ALL AUTHORS who so willingly agreed to have their words transcribed for this book, and the writers, who so willingly agreed to allow me to use, in some cases, significant portions of their articles or newsletters, are truly the people I must acknowledge first. Their wisdom appears in this book, which I hope will be useful to the reader. I have included their contact information as well, which I hope will be valuable to everyone who offered their insights for my use in this book.

I also feel indebted to GLOBAL TALK RADIO where these interviews took place. Without the station's constant support and encouragement, these programs would never have been as informative, entertaining and enjoyable for host and guests alike.

I tried to use some information or nugget of wisdom from everyone on my list. But, if I missed you, please know it was only due to the rigors of the manuscript's scope, and not through any lack of validity in your comments or writings. There is just so much to include, and just as with a film, some items go to the cutting room floor, even when they don't deserve to be left out.

My family has endured yet another seemingly endless project, and have patiently listened to my hemming and hawing about what to write here or what to put there. Their love and encouragement means more to me than they will ever know.

And, of course, I acknowledge all the authors I have been honored to serve as publisher. Without you, there would have been no reason to learn all this and no need to share it with anyone. I know the publishing road is uneven and pitted with potholes for most authors. We have all tried to make the best decisions as the opportunities have come along. This is a great adventure, and you and I embarked on it together. We will continue to travel together and find the best way to make the most of your books.

I am a believer in the power of the written word, and am humbled every morning when I sit down to work for you. I love my job, and it is because of you.

CONTENT

Endorsements
Dedication
Introduction
Acknowledgements

1. Who is your reader?	19
2. Genre—Who are you as an author?	34
3. Where will you find your audience?	46
4. Why you must Write, Edit, Re-write, and Re-edit	69
5. Can You Tell a Book by Its Cover?	93
6. How Hard Is It to Sell a Book?	107
7. How Will You Market Your Book?	124
8. Printing—Since the Gutenburg Bible	185
9. The Publishing Revolution—Knowledge Is Power	196
10. Reality Breaks the Mold—Setting Realistic Expectations	218
11. Press Releases & Better Press Coverage	235
12. The Essentials of the Internet	261
CONCLUSION	291
INDEX	295

Every great accomplishment begins with the decision to try.
—Anonymous

CALLING ALL AUTHORS

CHAPTER 1

Who is your reader?

Only a person with a Best Seller mind can write Best Sellers.
—Aldous Leonard Huxley, 1894-1963

Whenever I ask this question of a prospective author, "Who is your reader?" I am most often met with silence. So few authors think about who their readers actually are going to be, they miss the mark entirely. Children's book authors often write for small children using grown-up ideas and words. Fiction authors believe their readers will be like them, interested in a good story. But, a reader of Science Fiction is looking for satisfaction in a wholly different way than a reader of Romance novels. Mystery writers have a different sensibility to meet than Historical Fiction writers, and so on. And, when it comes to non-fiction, the width and breadth of variety is astronomical. If one leaves the academic books out of the equation, most non-fiction authors are interested first in selling their books, which in turn will sell their speeches, which in turn will sell their products. Simply said, the writing of the book itself is a labor that must be endured to attract the reader beyond the book. The pros and cons of writing books for sales purposes might merit another book to wage the arguments fairly. So, let's return to the first question the writer should ask him/herself: "Who is your reader?"

Some relatively lengthy period of time before the writer begins to write his book, he should seek out and discover the answer to The Question. Is your readership primarily women? If so, what demographic of women? Ten to seventeen year olds? Eighteen to twenty-four year old women? Thirty-something? Forty and up? Sixty and beyond? Professional women? Teachers? Stay-at-home Moms? Or, are you aiming your book at men. Again, what kind of men? Businessmen? Athletes? Computer geeks? Young, middle aged, older and wiser?

Can't answer the question? Most writers will hear the silence and then say, "Everyone who likes to read." Let me warn you right here. Not everyone is going to want to read your book. No matter how wonderful you think it is, or how wonderful your closest friends and family think it is, the alleys behind the book publishers', distributors' and wholesalers' warehouses are littered with bins filled with books that "everyone" didn't want to read. Frightening thought? Well, it should be. If a writer can't identify his readers, he is in real trouble when it comes to getting the book published and making back his investment of time and money.

"I don't care who reads it, I write for myself," is another reply I hear when I pose The Question. I believe this to be the ultimate cop-out reply. The author who commits this sort of egotism is going to find his book in the bins behind the warehouses, if it gets published at all. The Art for Art's Sake group of writers may still have some resonance in the literary world, but without a clear sense of who the readers will be, the publisher will have a hard time selling even the best written, most cleverly conceived, purely cast works to the voracious reading public. One must have a door upon which to knock if one is going to sell books.

Think for a moment about the door-to-door salesmen and women of a generation ago. Avon Cosmetics still uses the one-on-one approach, updated for the current day trends to be sure, to sell reasonably priced beauty aids to women in their homes. The Fuller Brush salesmen knew their market: women who wanted to please their families in every possible way, including having the best collection of brushes for every task. Vitamins, magazines, Bibles, Tupperware, all manner of fund-raising items for the local schools, and encyclopedias have all arrived on the unsuspecting doorstep with a clean-cut salesperson ready to offer the best item in the arsenal for a price. All these companies knew who their target market was, and if they survived for anytime at all, they appealed to that market by knowing what it wanted and provided the answer to the needs of the person who answered the door. Infomercials and shopping networks have mostly replaced the door-to-door sales person, but if you think about it, only the door has changed. The television and the internet Web site have become the entrance to the marketplace for all things, and most especially books.

So, again, "Who is your reader?" is the most important question an author can ask, before, during and after the book is written.

Look at Past and Present Best Sellers to Learn

The actual all-time list of the top ten best sellers is an amazing amalgam of titles, some predictable, some surprising. I have chosen ten other best-selling titles to analyze, but find the actual Top Ten of interest for the purposes of illustrating this concept: What is truly a best seller?

In Russell Ash's The Top 10 of Everything 2002, the author provides a list of the 10 bestselling books of all time. That list is provided in the following table. Note that several of the books have been published as annual editions.

Rank	Author	Book	Pub Date	Sales
1	Various	The Holy Bible	C.1451-55	More than 6 Billion
2	Mao Tse-Tung	Quotations from Chairman Mao	1966	900,000,000
3	Noah Webster	The American Spelling Book	1783	Up to 100,000,000
4	Mark C. Young	Guiness Book of World Records	1955	More than 90,000,000
5	World Almanac Edictor	World Almanac	1868	73,500,000
6	William Holmes McGuffey	The McGuffey Readers	1836	60,000,000
7	Benjamin Spock	The Common Sense Book of Baby and Child Care	1946	More than 50,000,000
8	Elbert Hubbard	A Message to Garcia	1899	More than 40,000,000
9	Charles Monroe Sheldon	In His Steps, What Would Jesus Do?	1896	More than 30,000,000
10	Jaqueline Susann	Valley of the Dolls	1966	More than 30,000,000

The following Top Ten list is this: Atlas Shrugged, The Bible, Harry Potter, the DaVinci Code, Chicken Soup for the Soul, Lord of the Rings, The Chronicles of Narnia, The Grinch

Who Stole Christmas, Tuesdays with Morrie, The Atkins Diet. You can make your own list, but, I have chosen these to illustrate the process you must take your own book through if you want to know who your reader is. The variety of genre here should give most writers a guide to follow. Answer the following five questions for your book, and you'll have a good idea who will want to read your book.

What single most important idea does the book offer to readers?

1. Atlas Shrugged: Objectivism
2. The Bible: Judeo/Christian philosophy
3. Harry Potter: Magic and Sorcery for Kids
4. The DaVinci Code: Controversy and a Puzzle for adults
5. Chicken Soup for the Soul: Comfort and Self-Help for everyone on many topics
6. Lord of the Rings: The ultimate magical war between Good and Evil
7. The Chronicles of Narnia: Magic, adventure and heroism
8. How The Grinch Stole Christmas: A lesson in generosity
9. Tuesdays with Morrie: How to value every stage of life
10. The Atkins Diet: Get thin and stay thin.

How does the reader put himself into the book's message?

1. Atlas Shrugged: Who is John Galt and why do you want to know? Because Objectivism teaches that it is good and right to be completely self-driven to succeed, it appeals to those who are tired of conforming to society's standards and demands.

2. **The Bible**: Useful for religious training and moral guidance in a world that seems lacking in both.

3. **Harry Potter**: Opens the imaginations of children using the ultimate power of Magic to bring triumph to Good over Evil, while entertaining everyone who reads it.

4. **The DaVinci Code**: Calls into question the most basic of Christian beliefs and places the reader in a position to figure out the mystery, all while entertaining the mind.

5. **Chicken Soup for the Soul**: When a person needs to turn to a book for inspiration and motivation, this series books reaches out to many looking for answers in the pop-culture.

6. **Lord of the Rings**: Tolkien's characters mirror the best and the worst in human beings. The reader finds himself in one or more of the characters and can live the story as if one with that character. Lessons of honor, loyalty and heroism are an added bonus.

7. **The Chronicles of Narnia**: C.S. Lewis adds richness, beauty, and depth to the nature of fantasy. His breathtaking and encouraging adventures for young and old reflect his own beliefs of faith and hope, good and evil, the truly miraculous and the miraculously true.

8. **How The Grinch Stole Christmas**: Everyone has known a Grinch. And everyone can feel the joy of the arrival Christmas, even without gifts. The warmth of the Grinch's transformation gives hope to

the reader that even the most selfish can become generous and caring.

9. **Tuesdays with Morrie**: No one would choose to die as Morrie died, but we all could choose to live as he lived. Mitch Albom lets us in on the gifts of wisdom Morrie gave to him as they came together for the last year of Morrie's life. That we all could be so lucky.

10. **The Atkins Diet**: One more attempt to lose the flab and become the svelt being the reader thinks he/she should be. A tried and true formula, not without risk, that one can perhaps live with for life.

What kind of person is looking for this book?

1. **Atlas Shrugged**: Adults who are tired of conforming to society's standards and demands.

2. **The Bible**: Churches, hotels, Christian families, Theological Seminaries.

3. **Harry Potter**: Children ages 10 and up.

4. **The DaVinci Code**: Adults who read for escape but like to think while they do it.

5. **Chicken Soup for the Soul**: Anyone who feels insecure, discouraged, or just needs a boost.

6. **Lord of the Rings:** Young adults and adults who love fantasy escape.

7. **The Chronicles of Narnia:** Children and adults who will read to them, teens and fantasy lovers of all ages.

8. **How The Grinch Stole Christmas:** Children and their parents who hope their children won't turn out to be Grinches.

9. **Tuesdays with Morrie:** Anyone entering their middle years.

10. **The Atkins Diet:** People unhappy with their silhouette.

What does the author's life bring to the book?

1. **Atlas Shrugged:** Ayn Rand lived her philosophy.

2. **The Bible:** Prophets and sages long dead cannot change the stories.

3. **Harry Potter:** J.K. Rowling was destitute, living in her car and wrote to stay sane. Who can't relate to that?

4. **The DaVinci Code:** Dan Brown carefully planned the controversy that drives the sales of the novel.

5. **Chicken Soup for the Soul:** Jack Canfield's great inspiration and motivational skills make the series timeless.

6. Lord of the Rings: Influences on the story of The Lord of the Rings, include philology, mythology and religion, as well as earlier fantasy works and Tolkien's experiences in World War I.

7. The Chronicles of Narnia: Lewis' family moved to a large house in the country when he was seven. The house contained long hallways and empty rooms, and Lewis and his brother invented make-believe worlds while exploring their home. Like Caspian and Tirian, Lewis lost his mother at an early age, and like Edmund, Jill, and Eustace, he spent a long, miserable time in English boarding schools.

8. How The Grinch Stole Christmas: Just like the Grinch, Theodor Geisel, (Dr. Seuss) didn't like participating in the celebrations of the holidays. The Grinch wasn't a villain to Dr. Seuss—just a guy whose heart, "two sizes too small," needed a therapeutic dose of the holiday spirit. In fact, Seuss identified with the fuzzy anti-hero.

9. Tuesdays with Morrie: Mitch Albom learns life's lessons from his professor from college, Morrie Schwartz. Mitch's discontent with life, career, and society is transformed as he visits his dying teacher whose unabashed zest for life to the very end provides the example.

10. The Atkins Diet: As an internist and cardiologist he developed the Atkins diet in the early 1970s. The diet is a ketogenic diet—a high protein, high fat, and very low carbohydrate regimen resulting in ketosis, a potentially harmful state which burns fat.

📖 Why will the reader recommend this book to others?

1. **Atlas Shrugged:** Intellectually, Objectivism creates an attractive alternative to the current way of living. The story engages the imagination and the message engages the heart.

2. **The Bible:** It is the ultimate source for all Christian belief.

3. **Harry Potter:** The success of the magical themes serves to engage children in the act of reading and draws them away from today's overtly technological games that can become obsessions.

4. **The DaVinci Code:** The controversial contentions in the story fuel the flames of argument, and one cannot argue intelligently if one hasn't read the book. So, it continues to sell.

5. **Chicken Soup for the Soul:** Anyone who reads a Chicken Soup for the Soul book knows others who will want to read it too.

6. **Lord of the Rings:** Tolkein is the master of the genre, and over time, if one hasn't read these works, then one remains illiterate in the fantasy genre.

7. **The Chronicles of Narnia:** These tales inspire the imagination, and childhood is the best time to open that door of a child's mind.

8. **How The Grinch Stole Christmas:** A timeless tale that translates to real life in an instant.

9. Tuesdays with Morrie: At one time or another, everyone questions the meaning of life, and tries to find it. This book helps the reader follow the path.

10. The Atkins Diet: Imitation is the truest form of flattery, and this diet has been imitated and modified by many others in the weight-loss field.

Once you have the portrait of your reader established, it is helpful to find out if that demographic actually exists in the marketplace. Here is how this exercise turns out for my first title **SACRED NIGHT**.

📖 **What single most important idea does the book offer to readers?**
There is no magic pill or potion that will guarantee a healthy old age. If there were, it would be exploited and bring ruin to all those who would use it for personal gain.

📖 **How does the reader put himself into the book's message?**
The universal theme of finding the fountain of youth in a pill or a potion is very seductive. Millions have tried every imaginable means of preserving youth, as the cosmetic surgery, Botox and diet industries all know. Billions are spent each year in the pursuit of retaining youth. And in the medical field, there are all those battling cancer, Alzheimer's, Parkinson's and other diseases of aging. Millions of readers fall into these demographics.

📖 What kind of person is looking for this book?

Readers who enjoy mystery, magic realism and a touch of romance will love this book. Anyone who fits the demographics of people wanting to stay young and fit at all cost will love this book.

📖 What does the author's life bring to the book?

Her father died of Alzheimer's. She lived in the Third World in her youth. She worked in the travel industry and has traveled extensively. As an educator, she taught French literature all her adult life. She brings her own first hand experience with aging diseases, imagery and aura from her Third World experiences and a powerful imagination to the task of building a three layer story. She weaves together the fantasy world, the real world and the Third World scenes with a masterful skill that uses Existential themes in the mystery genre.

📖 Why will the reader recommend this book to others?

This book keeps the reader engaged and wondering what will happen next, always trying to figure out who the antagonist really is, and ultimately because it is a satisfying tale that makes its point clearly and entertains the whole way.

📖 📖 📖

Now, you will need to put your book into this model to find who your reader is. Answer these five questions as honestly and dispassionately as you can. Then you will have a portrait of your reader, and the first defined idea of how your book can reach them effectively.

📖 What single most important idea does the book offer to readers?

_____
_____
_____
_____
_____
_____
_____
_____
_____

📖 How does the reader put himself into the book's message?

_____
_____
_____
_____
_____
_____
_____
_____
_____
_____

📖 What kind of person is looking for this book?

_____
_____
_____

📖 What does the author's life bring to the book?

📖 Why will the reader recommend this book to others?

📖 **NOTES:**

CHAPTER 2
Genre—Who are you as an author?

A book is a success when people who haven't read it pretend they have.
—Los Angeles Times Syndicate

During the first year of Calling All Authors, I discovered there were many more authors writing in unconventional genre than in the mainstream genre. Books about spirituality, religion, the paranormal, memoir fiction based on the author's life, how-to non-fiction to help parents pay for college, missionary life in Samoa, event books for children, religion as hatred, book promotion on a shoestring, dealing with the dying, autobiographies by twenty-something authors, children's books dealing with interracial families, and so on. Very often, the talking points included why the author chose his particular topic.

I have selected several authors' commentaries to transcribe here, and comment about these conversations to show how the reality of writing beyond the marketplace can produce interesting books that could certainly appeal to a wide audience.

Three O'Clock @ Hyde Park by Barbara Theesfeld is a romance novel focusing on a woman's inner beauty rather than her outer physical self.

"It is not everyday you can pick up a book and be engrossed from the first page...although it is a modern day love story, the real focus of the book is based on inner beauty and life recovery." Amazon.com review.

Barbara explains her book this way: "I wanted to have a theme running through the book...the thing that caught my attention in today's news, a lot of women suffer from body dismorphic dysfunction, the technical term for anorexia. When a woman looks into a mirror and sees a wrinkle or a couple of gray hairs, instead she sees a lot of gray hair, or a lot of wrinkles or a lot of blemishes...but [the image] is not really as bad as it seems...so our heroine is scarred from a car accident, and as a result she retreats into herself...she meets the hero, a bookshop owner and an average guy, on the internet...it's a very up-to-date story. The heroine is also a dietitian who is a closet junk-food junky...I used to work as a dietitian and know first hand how dietitians are about junk food...and when she is stressed out she goes for the cheese doodles and doughnuts...leaving a trail of coffee cups all over the house. She's very, very real, not like the typical romance heroine who has perfect hair and a fancy home...I decided I was going to keep my book clean and humorous...but not corny...but I use scenes where the reader can imagine what goes on...everyone can read it and not blush..."

I think Barbara did a wise thing by choosing to create her heroine with the foibles of so many women who are overtly and overly self-critical. I related to the idea right away and could see how a majority of women in America could relate as well. She consciously left out explicit sex scenes and chose to use the power of the imagination instead. Putting humor into the book and keeping the characters 'real' are two more choices that allow the reader to connect with the tale. In a world overwhelmed by sex and murder in romance novels, how refreshing it is to find a romance novel that focuses elsewhere.

John Henderson's book Fear, Faith, Fact and Fantasy deals "with the harmful effects of religion and how religion has interfered so much historically with philosophy, with medicine, with science and even with establishing human morality. Religions have always been on either side of whatever moral issue that you wanted to bring up, so people who say that religion causes man to be moral are absolutely wrong...in fact, I think that the Muslim religion is probably 300 years behind the Christian religion, at least for the last 200 or 300 years we have not been killing people in the name of the Christian God. We may shun them, we may excommunicate them, we may be intolerant of them, but we normally don't kill them."

When I commented about the Crusades being over, John replied, "[The Crusades] are not over for the Muslims. And I think that anybody thinks that they're going to be able to get the Sunnis and the Shiites to establish a democracy in Iraq, they need to go back and look at history a little closer...the chances of that happening are not very great...let's hope they will establish a government that can hold it all together...but historically no one has been able to do in the Near East that since Ataturk

[who] was able to establish some semblance of a democracy in Turkey by putting religion back in the churches, synagogues and the mosques...the same [is true] in this country, unless we put religion back into the home and the churches, we'll continue fighting over women's rights, homosexuality and things of that nature, where you find that somebody's God is on each side of the fence..."

I commented about Greek and Roman gods and how they have been reduced from viable religious deities to mythological entities with no theological power. John continued to clarify:

"This book is about what is fantasy and what is reality in religion...I thought this needed to be said in a more humanistic perspective...to [help some people] get over their guilt of giving up their childhood beliefs. I've had several people come up to me and say, 'I'm so glad you wrote this book, Dr. Henderson, because when I refused to be baptized as a teenager I was told I was going to go to Hell.'

"It will help some people get over their fear of death...the fear of death really bugs people. If they would realize they had no fear of nothingness before they were born, and there's no reason to believe there is going to be anything, at least as we experience life, after you're dead, then they can get over that terrible fear of Death [and] a Supernatural Being who is keeping close records on us and then who is going to tally it all up at the end and send us to Heaven or to Hell...

"As Science progresses and our knowledge progress, on the other hand, organized religions are very powerful. They will not allow books like mine or they will end up being burned. A librarian told me that my book had been taken out—not checked out—of the library and not returned. This is the way they keep people from thinking about the subject.

"As Martin Luther said, 'To be a Christian, you must tear the eyes out of Reason.' Once an individual starts to think and reason, then much of what is written in the Bible, obviously is not true...there is almost nothing original in Christianity...even the Golden Rule was known long before Christianity...even the miracles and the Immaculate Conception and the Resurrection have been in dozens of religions before Christianity."

The controversial ideas that fill Dr. Henderson's books clearly spawn a response from readers, both good and bad. Stirring up controversy is one of the best ways to sell books, and yet, one publisher rejected this book saying "As a no-name author writing on a subject like this, you are wasting your time." But, Dr. Henderson felt like it had to be said from a humanistic perspective, [even though] it has been said before in other ways. He exudes more confidence, knowledge about his topic, and courage to get his message across than many authors do.

Dr. Henderson's books are available online at Amazon.com, B&N.com and other online stores.

John Washburn's novel When Evils Prospers takes on the negative trends and changes in American society and is a fictional tale that in reality is "a call to action for Americans to unite for the betterment of our nation."

"I see an America has become something our founding fathers may not have intended, that has drifted for the worse. The message is that I think we've gotten too far away from the original vision of our democracy...that was placed in the Constitution. And, I think we need to pause for a second and think about getting back to basics."

I commented about how people are blind-sided by agenda-driven judges, and how in the real basics of how people are on the street, it is the older people who smile and say hello, while the younger people couldn't be bothered. It's everything from the political agenda issues to general treatment of each other. "How do you react to the charges of right-wing extremism in the book?"

"I have gotten some of that. The first person who reviewed the book said it was too political with too much political commentary. I don't consider it right-wing. There is political commentary superimposed on a fictional setting, but to me it is more traditional than right-wing…I describe myself as a traditional nationalist. Traditional as our fore-fathers intended. Nationalist meaning America first, always…It may appear right wing, because granted so much of the right-wing base is traditional. When did traditional values become extremist? This book is not meant to endorse any right-wing party. I'm not too happy with any party right now…it makes for a good debate."

I commented about the controversy being a good way to market. "In the book, one of the characters makes the prediction that America will not survive the War on Terror. Yikes! Do you believe that?"

"That's my fear. I see it as a possibility. I don't believe a culture war can go on within our country at the same time we're trying to fight a global war on terror. I don't see how we can do it divided. If you've watched the last two elections, if there's one thing you see, it's division. And, that's the biggest concern. I think eventually we would succumb in one way or another if we didn't unite, and it makes me sad to say that. I'm a true patriot… but I don't see a good outcome unless we change our mindset as a nation. Think of it this way: if we were this divided in 1941 and had gone against the Nazis and the Imperialist Japanese, there's no doubt in my mind that we would have been defeated. I see that we're up against an enemy that is similar in strength and motivation, and we're doing it with a lot of bickering back and forth."

I commented that with today's technology we have more ways to expose our differing points of view, but in 1941 the everyday man didn't have a way to express his viewpoints beyond his small circle. So, I said, "And I think you're right that if we are divided in our awareness of what our enemy is out to do—when Armageddon is their goal—we need to sit up and take notice. What is the biggest threat at this time and is this threat portrayed in your book?"

"In my opinion, our biggest threat, our biggest enemy is ourselves. I don't see a nation, an army that can stand toe-to-toe with us and can conquer us when we are at full strength. But, we are divided, and in my mind the biggest threat is the politically progressive mindset and it is the reason we have drifted so far from the ideals of our founding fathers…So many of the problems we face today come out of the progressive mindset and how we have gotten away from the Constitution…A lot of the commentary in the book is geared this way…to help the reader see the possibilities. It is disturbing, and our future may not be so bright, if we don't open our eyes what's going on. I want America to see how far we've drifted from…our roots and dreams. How much further can we drift until we self-destruct… The point of no return is visible on the horizon."

I commented that the President in the book is female. "Is this an allusion to anyone in particular?"

"The character herself, the first female President, she is a left-wing political character. I have combined many bits and pieces of many national left-wing leaders [to build] this character."

John Washburn fills his book with controversy and when some reality of place and people in the fictional storyline, it is a good way to sell fiction. The questions his book poses are powerful, disturbing and potentially will be answered in the negative. All that makes for compelling reading.

John Washburn's books are available online at <u>Amazon. com</u>, <u>B&N.com</u> and many other online stores.

Zara Griswold's book **Surrogacy Was the Way** is based on the real-life stories of mothers who had their children via surrogacy, and also tells her own experience with having her twins via surrogacy.

"The guidebooks [while very informative] weren't what I was looking for…I really wanted to hear other people's stories, to learn what they went through and to feel like I wasn't alone. My book is geared toward intended mothers, because the woman is the one losing the chance to carry a baby, and because girls are raised to think they're going to have babies someday. Also, I wanted to make it for those thinking of being a surrogate. Also, it is meant to be useful for the doctors and nurses, fertility and egg-donor agencies, therapists and psychologists, [probably a thousand or more clinics in the United States, including all the doctors working in each clinic]. I hope that anyone suffering from infertility will see that surrogacy is an option. I didn't write this book to try to "sell" surrogacy, [no] to try and tell people that this is the way to create their families. I wrote for people to see there are options beyond adoption. And with the popularity of celebrities having children via surrogacy, it has become more commonplace...I don't want to sugarcoat the prospects, it doesn't always work out perfectly, I wanted people to see there can be many bumps along the way as well. I wasn't interested in telling only my story...I felt it was only one story and I wanted to show the variety of circumstance that lead to making this choice."

Go to www.zaragriswold.npauthors.com or www.surrogacywastheway.com for more information.

Michael Stadther is a self-publishing author who developed a new genre of books—event books. He met with profound rejection from the publishing community, and undaunted went on to create one of the most innovative series of books to come along in a long time.

A Treasure Trove and The Secrets of the Alchemist Dar, which both have a treasure hunt that go along with the books, Michael wants to draw the reader into the event (the prizes are millions of dollars worth of jewels) through the illustrated stories. His stories have brought families together by creating the puzzles that intrigued children and adults alike. He tied jewels into the story lines, so he had to contact jewelers to make the prizes, some hundreds of thousands of dollars per items (a $480,000 spider, for example), and he spread the jewel tokens all over the United States with the first book, and all over the world with the second book. The clues in the stories lead the reader to places where the tokens are hidden, and some people travel great distances and endure hardships to find them. There is even a solution manual for the extra tokens that he announced after the book was mostly solved. He leaves unsolved items unsolved for readers to continue to seek them.

This created buzz on the internet, with chat rooms where possible solutions were shared by people all over the country. These items are not on private property or in dangerous locations. Everyone in the world will have the same chance to get one of the hundred diamond rings through an even more mysterious clues this year.

Michael reads to 200 schools each year for no charge, all over the world, to spread the word about his books, the treasure hunt, and ultimately to encourage children to read. Those who look for the treasures are called Trovers, and in the second book the same characters return, but the new bad guy is Dar, the bad fairy. He wants to get the rings around the fairies' necks which keep the wearer safe, and they never get old and never die. It is a world-wide hunt for a hundred diamond rings, one of which is worth a million dollars. These are the most expensive books ever written. Three million dollars for the first book and six millions dollars for the second book.

Michael hasn't made a profit, but, he is having fun! He has fifteen people working for him in Connecticut, a studio of artists doing the illustrations, PR firms in New York, London and Australia, and he goes on a worldwide tour to launch the book around the world. After the launch tour, he does the school reading program the rest of the year. His background is in software and business, not writing, but something about treasure, hunt and jewels appeals to both boys and girls.

Michael explains his experience: "I was rejected by most of the big publishers, sometimes quite brutally. One involved a two page letter telling me they didn't like my writing, my illustrations, and that it was a horrible idea and I should never send this manuscript out to any publisher. So I have that one framed… Publishers are quite busy, but I was contacted by Jack Romanoff, the CEO of Simon and Schuster. He said, 'We rejected you. We were wrong, and let's do business together.' They help us with the layout of the books, they are our worldwide distributor, and do the printing, and I buy the jewels, so all the risk is borne on my shoulders."

The books have spawned Treasure Trove Inc. Michael did the first illustrations, but now has PR and marketing firms, a POD firm called www.everyonegetspublished.com with editing and stylistic help for new authors. He has people working for him who took a cut in salary to come work with him.

Michael's advice for first time authors looking for publishers: "Be persistent. Try to get your manuscript as polished as you can, even if you have to pay a little bit. Spend as much time writing your synopsis as you would two pages of your manuscript. If you don't, it doesn't reflect positively on your book. Agents have so much swamping them, so there are alternatives. Get out and talk about your book. This sells books. With the internet today, publishers connect writers and readers without a lot of stuff in the middle. You do have to tell a good story and craft your sentences very well."

Go to Michael's Web site, www.alchemistsdar.com to find out more.

The quest for your genre, the form in which you will expose your voice as an author, is probably the hardest part of a writer's job. Some writers are so easily convinced that there is no need to heed the requirements of the marketplace that they make their work forever unavailable to their potential audience. It is good to employ tried and true themes, which are the ultimate intrigue of the story. Yet, each author mentioned here has taken the tried and true and put his or her own stamp on it to make their books appealing beyond the commonplace. That is a smart step, and I highly recommend that you, as a writer, consider the marketplace and your book's place in it before you begin to write. We will deal with this concept again in coming chapters.

CHAPTER 3
Where will you find your audience?

A man really writes for an audience of about ten persons. Of course if others like it, that is clear gain. But if those ten are satisfied, he is content.
—Alfred North Whitehead, 1861-1947

It is essential, but not enough to know who your reader is. Knowing how to reach your reader is equally, if not more important. One of the most difficult aspects of publishing a book for the author is the frustration that looms large on the horizon as sales wane and the silence becomes deafening. The flurry of excitement fades fast just as soon as the friends and family have purchased the book, the book signing at the local bookstore has occurred and everyone has gone home. The letdown is strong, and the confusion new authors feel sets in.

Publishers hear this question often: "Why isn't my book selling anywhere?" The title is listed on all the online bookstores, the author's own Web site, the publisher's Web site. Sometimes, even the local bookstore has some on the shelves.

So much depends on the pre-publication planning where the reviews, publicity and email campaigns, press releases and follow up calls that get the mentions into the papers, onto the media wires and all over the internet is organized.

Most new authors do not understand the timeline their books must go through to even have a chance at being visible and therefore, purchased. Several important elements go into the pre-publication planning phase of a book's life, whether the author is self-published, has an independent publisher, or even if his book is being published by one of the largest publishers in the country. There is only so much time that a book has to make a name for itself, and that window of time is often missed by most authors. If you are published by a big house, the window is about six weeks. If you are published by a smaller firm, the window can be about three to six months. If you are self-published, it may take a year or more. Honestly, there is no strict rule here. Many books are creatively marketed for years. They take on a life of their own. But this longevity comes from wise and careful pre-publication planning.

Like many first-time authors, I made the mistake of thinking the order of events for my first book was: write, publish and publicize. It is quite the opposite: Publicize, write and publish. Actually, writing and publicizing can overlap quite a bit, but the date of publication should *never* precede the publicizing of the book.

But, to whom will you publicize your book? Where will you find the crowd who will line up at your book signings? Of course, your immediate friends, colleagues, family and local media can all be brought together at least once. But what about after that?

At first, it is embarrassing to publicize yourself and your book. This is a feeling you must get over very quickly. There is no modesty in promotion. You must get used to talking about yourself and your book with the confidence of a true believer, whether in press releases or emails, or as you line up signings or lectures. You must make friends with your extrovert personality and bring it out into the sunshine. You cannot succeed at booksignings or on interviews or give talks at libraries or schools without that "other part of who you are" to entertain the masses. Okay, sometimes the masses are really five or six people, but they deserve the best you have to give. If they all buy your book, being at the event is worth your time and theirs.

Most authors naïvely believe that their book will sell mega millions of copies all by itself. It seems like that's how it's done. Look at all the books on the best seller lists. They seem to magically climb the charts to fame and fortune, bringing the author's bank account right along with them. I recall thinking that any publisher I would want to give my book to for publishing would also want to do all the publicity and marketing. I even hired an agent, who did nothing by the way. I thought I could just sit back and let the money roll in.

That was before I researched publishers, tried the long and tedious query letter route to rejection, and finally, three years after the book had been written and edited, decided to become a publisher for my own books (more on this in a later chapter). If they weren't going to do the job, then I'd just have to do it myself. I bought my ISBNs, established the publishing entity named Nightengale Press, chose a printer connected to the industry leaders, registered as a DBA in my county and state, and I was in business.

Once the book was printed and in my hand, the first three times I set out to approach my local Borders store to try to set up a book signing, I sat in the parking lot and battled the inner voices that wanted me to give up right there. They won twice. I won the third time. After a period of time waiting, following up, walking in unexpectedly to talk with the manager about his decision to do or not to do the signing, and just being very politely persistent, he and I decided that because I was a teacher, we'd schedule the signing on the first Saturday during Teacher Appreciation Week. I put announcements in the school paper, on the daily PA announcements, and stuffed a flyer provided by the Borders in every teacher and staff mailbox in the district. I contacted the local journalist who covered school news and a feature article appeared in the paper the week before the signing. My students came, my colleagues came, my friends and family came, and the local papers took photos and did a follow-up article.

We sold eighty books in three hours. Eighty. The average is ten. It was a superb success, and I was able to do signings there and at other Borders stores in the area every month over a period of two years. I got to know several managers, and they were wonderful about supporting me and the authors I began to publish. I expanded this outreach to the Barnes and Noble stores in the area too. Who says the big guys won't touch a local author? Many of the stores actually welcome and help promote the local authors in the area, as long as the store makes money from the relationship.

It is possible to consistently sell twenty-five or thirty books per signing, but it takes developing and perfecting the skills of approaching, engaging, informing and charming the customers as they come in the door. It takes a gimmick that changes with each signing. No sitting back behind a table and waiting for the public to approach. You must go out and reel them in. This takes courage. The skills can be learned, and actually it all becomes fun and entertaining for the author who genuinely likes people.

📖 The Bull's Eye Approach to Finding Your Target Audience

So, the first signing is a great success. Then what? I have learned that finding and developing your audience is a process that is reminiscent of a bull's eye. Think of yourself as the center of the target: the author (A) in the Bull's Eye. You are the first believer in your book. The first ring (1) is your immediate circle of friends and colleagues. These people turn out once. The second ring (2) is your immediate local area, your town library, your town bookstore, your local schools, your chamber of commerce, your local reading groups, the public access television station, and the local small watt radio station. These are all excellent places to give interviews, talks and signings about how you wrote your book and published your book. If there is anything in your book that reflects your local area, so much the better.

The third ring of the target (3) is the state you live in. The fourth (4) ring is the region where your state is located. The fifth (5) ring is the nation and the outside ring (6) is the world. Each ring has an audience waiting to hear from you, and you can build outward from the center as you saturate each ring of the target. Each ring of your target market has similar sources for you to reach your audience.

Planning how you are going to reach your audience in each of the sectors in the target takes vision, time, persistence, on-going investment, boundless energy and help. No one can do this entirely alone.

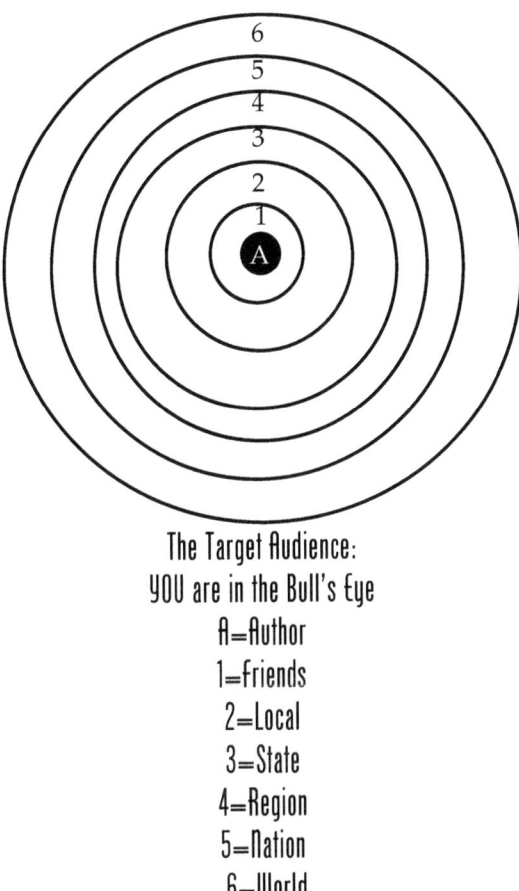

The Target Audience:
YOU are in the Bull's Eye
A=Author
1=Friends
2=Local
3=State
4=Region
5=Nation
6=World

Your publisher will help in some ways, but the honest truth is, the publisher's job in promotion is relatively limited. An initial press release, the author Web site, help entering tradeshows, award programs and co-op advertising, and working with bookstores you have already contacted is the minimum. Helping you find a publicist and get some reviews perhaps. You'll get to do the email campaigns, the media contacts, the door-to-door face-to-face time with managers and journalists, and all the other more labor-intensive items on the list.

📖 Going Outside Your Comfort Zone

To set up your appearance schedule, your reviews and your press releases, you should remember, that doing so after your book is released makes getting any reviews other than paid review service reviews much harder, if not impossible. Reviews do not actually sell books, but they help get events lined up. Press releases do not sell books, but they help get events lined up. Newspaper articles do not sell books, but they help bring the public to your events. To earn the articles, you must be doing something newsworthy. To make press releases useful, you must do something newsworthy. To get reviews you must send your manuscript or galley book to reviewers who may be interested in reviewing it well before the publication date. Six months before is about right. Four months before is tight. Most review sources list submission guidelines on their Web sites.

What do you do when your book is already published and the local markets have been exhausted? So many authors and publishers wonder, "How can PR be affordable?"

Maryglenn McCombs, owner of Maryglenn McCombs Book Publicity (www.maryglenn.com) addresses these questions with eight steps authors and publishers can take to create "buzz" and how to think outside the book.

"The media is a powerful factor in the reader's decision to buy or to not buy a book. Buzz is about recognition and familiarity, word of mouth, conversation about the book. Buzz is the sound of book groups talking about a book. It is the sound of the author's voice on radio and television. Buzz is the sound of boxes of books being packed, shipped and opened to be sold. Buzz is re-orders and re-prints. Buzz is the sound of a successful book.

"Timing is everything. Having plenty of lead time is essential when you are launching a new book. Many PR campaigns begin before the final edits are complete and long before the final touches have been made to a book's cover design. A great deal of advance planning goes into a book launch. Galleys (ARCs—advance review copies) are distributed to reviewers well in advance of when books are available in stores. These are received four to five months before the book will be released. Mainstream magazines typically operate on a four to six month and sometimes longer lead time. In mid-May they are looking for Holiday ideas. Patience and planning in publishing are virtues.

"Overnight success is a misnomer in the publishing business. Buyers often order books six to nine months before they are actually available. Often buyers from larger chains and independent stores place orders based on titles, concept and cover design alone. Printed, bound and finished books are not even in existence yet.

"Start your book's promotion by setting a publication date. A pub date is the official release, usually six weeks after the book comes off the press. It is a phantom date and is an approximate of when a book will be available in stores. It functions as a means to coordinate media placements and in-store availability and tying the book promotion and distribution together, sometimes to coordinate with a particular time of year. You should set the pub date to allow more time than you ever think you will need to promote your book."

📖 Maryglenn's Eight Points to Book Promotion Success:

📖 **Get specific and resist the urge to mass mail.** Customize your pitch to the specific media.

📖 **View your role as helping the journalist,** not the journalist helping you.

📖 **Write your own buzz** by writing articles for journalists to use.

📖 **Research editorial calendars** that detail specific features, articles and themes, often available on the magazine Web sites.

📖 **Have at least three pitch ideas in mind.** If your first pitch about a booksigning doesn't work, try your second: an article about the author. If that doesn't work, use the third, a feature story about how the book is relevant to an issue in the local area.

📖 **Keep an open mind about media outlet.** No media outlet is too small.

📖 **Start where you are and remember where you were.** Even alumni periodicals, hometown papers and local media.

📖 **Make media equal sales.** Give bookstores a reason to sell your book. Let the stores know when an author is appearing on a show or article in a particular area. Give them a reason to order and stock your books.

"Be patient, keep a sense of humor, enjoy the process, be ready to take chances, and don't be discouraged when the process takes time."

📖 CHILDREN'S BOOKS—Special Genre Requires Special Approach

"Florrie Binford Kichler of Patria Press, Inc., is the publisher of the Young Patriots series. Go to www.patriapress.com for more about her books and her press. The following is excerpted from her April 2006 article in the PMA Independent.

"Making money with bookstores is the challenge. Most children's book publishers do need bookstores for sales and credibility. In my experience, however, the key to a healthy bottom line is not relying on bookstores as the major source of income—those pesky returns will get you every time. Stepping outside the traditional channel for selling children's books can net you big rewards in terms of both large and small nonreturnable sales. Nonreturnable—a lovely word. And what about getting paid in 30 days instead of 60, 90, or more?

📖 **Launch a four-pronged attack on nontraditional channels**: associations, book clubs, museums/historic sites, and schools.

📖 ASSOCIATIONS

"The Encyclopedia of Associations (both a database and a print source) lists more than 100,000 membership organizations. Odds are excellent that at least one or two of them have a mission that would dovetail perfectly with the subject matter of any given book. Do you have a title about pets or animals? Try the ASPCA. Sports? Check the "Athletic and Sport" category. Is your children's book educational? Category (05), "Education," may have a perfect match. If your book has a religious theme, look through the entries for "Religious" (11).

"Once you have a list of prospects, how can you get their attention?

📖 **Learn about an association's mission,** structure, board of directors, and executive director...which you will be able to glean from the association's Web site—to craft a proposal that emphasizes over and over again how your book will help it and its members. In the course of writing a proposal to a large national association for one of my titles, I pointed out how my book would help it achieve its goals in terms of every single sentence in its mission statement.

📖 **What kind of offer do you make?** The only limit is your imagination—and what you learned in your research about an organization. For instance, an association can use your books as:

- 📖 an incentive to get members to join or renew
- 📖 a product for its online bookstore
- 📖 a gift as part of an educational seminar
- 📖 a fundraiser

📖 **Your offer should focus on ownership while adding value and subtracting cost.** Treat the organization as your partner, not just your customer—you want it to be vested in the project so that the staff sees your book as their book and thus will continue to order year after year.

📖 **Include a custom cover** with the organization's logo,

📖 **[Place] a couple of pages in the front matter** with a message from its executive director

📖 **[Provide] bookmarks** that use the design for your own bookmarks but add the group's logo.

📖 **Offer to donate a percentage** of book sales revenue back to the organization

📖 **Set an attractive price** for the association's quantity purchase but keep a profit margin you can live with.

📖 **Donate 15 percent back to the organization** for each copy members[buy] through the association.

📖 **Don't underprice.** No matter how anxious you are to make the sale, remember that you have content the group needs (you have shown them specifically why they need it). Set your price high enough to include a decent profit and to allow for some negotiating room. Allow much more time than you think you'll need. These kinds of sales can take more than a year to accomplish.

📖 BOOK CLUBS

"There is a book club for every conceivable interest, including any interest a child may have. Book club sales are similar to association sales as they generally involve large quantities of books sold nonreturnable, but the discount requirements can be much greater—80 percent is not unusual. For our purposes, we'll define book clubs as actual clubs that mail books to their members as well as large companies that sell books in nontraditional, nonretail outlets, such as schools, hospitals, and corporations.

"Two large book clubs for children's titles are the **Children's Book-of-the-Month Club** and **Junior Library Guild**. Both work on a membership model, with Junior Library Guild targeting librarians and Children's BOMC focusing on consumers. Both require submissions well in advance of your book's publication—at least a year ahead, in fact, which means you will likely be submitting manuscripts with artwork if you have it...and focus on benefits. You may indeed have the greatest children's book in the universe with the most beautiful illustrations, but what the clubs want to know is why their particular members will buy it.

"Two of the better-known entities that sell children's books in nonstore venues are **Books Are Fun** and **Scholastic Book Clubs**. Both employ a two-step process, first testing your book and then, if the test goes well, ordering thousands or even tens of thousands of copies.

📖 Advantages of Book Club Sales:

- 📖 Large quantities
- 📖 No returns
- 📖 Lower unit cost when you add a club's order to your own print run,
- 📖 The cachet that comes from including "a selection of the Such-and-Such Club" on all your marketing materials.

"The downside is the pricing; with gigantic quantities come huge discount requirements, so be careful what you wish for. Crunch the numbers to leave some profit, and be sure you have the infrastructure in place to deliver the 80,000 copies you promise.

📖 MUSEUMS

"A 2005 Association of Children's Museums Membership Survey found that more than 30 million children and families visit children's museums annually. That's a lot of potential book buyers for just one segment of this potentially lucrative and evergreen market. Depending on the topic of your book, museums and historic sites can be profitable outlets. There is a multitude of types of museums, and once again, creativity is key in determining where to place your children's book. Children's museums and modern science museums are an obvious starting point, but remember, parents bring children to art museums, natural history museums, botanical gardens, state history museums, battlefields, U.S. history museums—the list goes on and on.

Resources That Can Help You Find Museums

American Association of Museums (www.aam-us.org/index.cfm)
Museum Store Association (www.museumdistrict.com)
Official Museum Directory (www.nationalregisterpublishing.com)

Eastern National, the major distributor to federal historic sites and National Parks shops (see the list of more than 150 bookstores that it distributes to at www.easternnational.org, and contact the company by phone or email for specific guidelines for submitting review copies).

"Again, it is crucial to target your prospects and focus on what your book will do for their customers.

SCHOOLS

"Sales to the school market are a topic for an article in and of themselves—in fact, entire books have been written on the subject—so I will focus on one of my favorite aspects of the subject, the school visit. Authors are the best ambassadors for their books, and nearly every school has some kind of writing event, writing program, or course of study that lends itself to a visiting author program.

"The major advantage of school visits is that they often result in a double whammy in terms of revenue. The school may order books for its library and/or classrooms, and it may also give the author the opportunity to sell books to individual children and teachers on the day of the event. Plus, the author gets a speaking fee.

"Create a flyer in advance for teachers to send home with their students (always with permission, of course). In the flyer, we generally provide a discount to the buyer

"Offer to donate one book to the school's library for every 10 books sold—added value in terms of an incentive without much added cost. And since these are direct sales, you will net a relatively large portion of cover price even after the small discount.

Advantages of School Sales

- No returns
- More income
- A speaking fee
- Creating goodwill

"Add it up, and you'll quickly realize why school visits can be a lucrative component of your children's-book sales."

Give yourself a fair amount of time to deal with each sector in the target. This timeline can be from six months to a year per sector, and as you are winding up one sector, you should already have the next one in motion. Remember, there is no such thing as an overnight success. It takes dedication and hard work. Plan it all out ahead of publication and you will have a far better chance to find your audience.

📖 PLAN YOUR BULL'S EYE TARGET MARKET

Your Name:
Your Book's Title:
Your Book's Genre:
Your Reader Portrait:

ZONE A - THE AUTHOR IS YOU
Describe yourself, your personality, your willingness to go outside your comfort zone, your contacts who can help you publicize your book.

_____
_____
_____
_____
_____
_____
_____
_____
_____
_____
_____
_____
_____
_____
_____
_____
_____
_____
_____

📖 ZONE 1 - YOUR FRIENDS

List your friends, those who will be interested in buying your book at signings, telling their friends about you and your book, anyone who can help to connect with local media or organizations where you can talk about your book.

_____
_____
_____
_____
_____
_____
_____
_____
_____
_____
_____
_____
_____
_____
_____
_____
_____
_____
_____
_____
_____
_____
_____
_____
_____
_____

ZONE 2 - YOUR LOCAL AREA

List all media outlets in your town and surrounding towns. If you are near a large city, include radio, TV and print media there as well. Include contact names, Web site, phone numbers. Guidelines for submission of press releases and story proposals should be gathered from these sources. Include libraries, bookstores, community organizations, schools and colleges, too.

📖 ZONE 3 - YOUR STATE

Expand your contact list to places farther from home, still in your state, or if you live near the state line, into communities near the border in the neighboring state. You are still looking for all the same outlets.

_____
_____
_____
_____
_____
_____
_____
_____
_____
_____
_____
_____
_____
_____
_____
_____
_____
_____
_____
_____
_____
_____
_____
_____
_____
_____
_____
_____
_____

📖 ZONE 4 - YOUR REGION

Expand your contact list to places farther from your state to the other states in your region. You are still looking for all the same kinds media and community outlets, just in other states in your part of the country.

_____
_____
_____
_____
_____
_____
_____
_____
_____
_____
_____
_____
_____
_____
_____
_____
_____
_____
_____
_____
_____
_____
_____
_____
_____
_____
_____
_____

📖 ZONE 5 - NATION

Now you are expanding to the major metorpolitan markets, using the same process as for your state and your region. The smaller markets outside the metropolitan areas will follow what the major media outlets

ZONE 6 - GLOBAL

Expand your reach to the global markets using a combinaiton of the internet and the radio, TV and print media leaders in foreign countries. Start with English-speaking countries, and if you can, expand from there.

📖 Success in Expanding Your Market is Hard Work

As you begin this process of building your market, remember the first group will help you get started. You will learn your particular promotional style right at home with your friends and in your local marketplace. As you gain confidence, making the phone calls, writing the press releases, setting up events, doing the events, giving talks, submitting articles, and all the other tasks that help bring attention to you and your book, you will see sales occuring. Sales come from many areas, not just the internet or the bookstore signing. Every avenue you take will teach you something, and even the unsuccessful efforts provide valuable lessons to learn.

Begin your planning before your book is written. Work consistently and persistently. Never give up promoting your book. When you do that, you doom it to oblivion. So, even when the going gets tough, you know the old line—"the tough get going." I'd put it this way: "When the going gets tough, the tough KEEP going." I have taught this and lived this ethic all my life. Nothing is ever over until you quit. So, here is the motto I live by:

BELIVE in yourself.
You can achive EXCELLENCE if you do these things:
WORK HARDER than others think is necessary.
EXPECT MORE OF YOURSELF than others think is possible.
CARE MORE about your success than others think is wise.
TAKE RISKS more than others think is prudent.
DREAM MORE than others think is practical, and,
NEVER, EVER QUIT!

CHAPTER 4
Why you must write, edit, re-write, and re-edit.

The difference between the right word and the almost right word is the difference between lightning and the lightning bug.
—Mark Twain [Samuel Langhorne Clemens], 1835-1910

It isn't enough to write a book. It isn't enough to give your manuscript to a friend to read and ask them to be your editor. Skill in writing is hard-earned. Any skill takes practice, error, correction, more practice, more error, more correction.

Compare the task of learning to write to learning to play the piano. Most people take piano lessons as children first and typically quit taking lessons in less than two years, largely because the work of learning to play the piano is tedious, unforgiving and time consuming. Those with natural musical 'talent' and whose parents are determined that the talent be fed may make it five or more years in formal lessons during childhood and the teenage years. Those who actually become performers and continue with piano lessons for more than ten years are rare. Students in music conservatories or full-time music programs in the university setting remain in the minority of students on any given campus. And, in the end, those who make a living and become well-known as musicians are even fewer and farther between in the general population of workers. The popular example of this truism lies in the reality that the

American Idol scouts screen over fifty thousand applicants to find twelve who will go to Hollywood. The odds for those who are without talent and training are enormous. Yet, fifty thousand people show up to try and twelve are chosen and one wins the contest.

So, you want to be a writer?

As I was working out at the gym one morning, another woman came into the room and began her workout. We were both able to talk through the exercise, and as it happened, she asked what I did for a living. I explained I was a publisher of books.

Her first response was: "I have always wanted to write a book! You know, an inspirational/motivational book—with the experience I have had in life, well, it would be great to help others."

Yes, many have the same thought, but this is not the clearest reason for becoming a writer, and I sensed her thought about being a writer was fleeting. What are some reasons people express that they want to write?

- to share a life story
- to provide advice and information
- to entertain
- to teach
- to make a living
- just to do it

Because I am a writer and I also publish books, often for first-time writers, I am frequently asked, "How does a person start writing?" The answer is so simple, yet so hard: "Start with the first word on the first page."

📖 It is really not that simple.

Writing requires discipline. You must set a time when you will write every day, no matter what happens in life. Just like practicing the piano, if you write every day, you will grow as a writer. Your skills will increase.

Jan Nathan of the Publisher's Marketing Association has this advice for writers:

"Using one's experience… even with fiction based on fact, don't try to put yourself into a place you've never been before or give yourself a voice you've never heard before because the writing will be very stilted and the book will never sell. But, if you share information that people need and you have some good practical advice, you have a good chance for success in this world today."

📖 It helps a lot if you make your writing time like a job where your boss is watching.

Of course, you are your own boss, and because we are human and our nature may be to slack off when we feel like doing something else, you must be strict with yourself. Also, you should reward your good behavior with something you like when you accomplish your goal. As a kid, when I was learning to play the piano, the reward was being able to go play with my friends after I had completed my practicing. Today, I reward myself by playing with my dog when I complete a chapter or going to lunch with a friend or dinner with my husband when I complete a writing project.

📖 Commit to writing for a set amount of time every day.

One hour? Two? Whatever you decide, you must write or be sitting at the computer ready to write at the pre-determined time for the pre-determined amount of time. Put some soft instrumental music on, turn off the ringer on the home phone, turn off your cell phone, be sure someone is watching the children, and then close the door. Make an environment where you are alone with the computer, the ideas and the time to write.

📖 Be sure to research anything in your book that others might not find believable.

Whether fiction or non-fiction, if your "facts" are wrong, the believability of the book dissolves as soon as anyone sees them as false.

Exception: the DaVinci Code—Dan Brown's research contributed to the controversy that went on to sell over 400 million copies by setting up a huge international discussion of whether or not his premise could be true, or was plagiarized. Good for him. Would that we could all do that!

📖 To make an outline—or not to make an outline, that is the question.

Some authors do, some don't. It is very important to have a vision of where the story starts, develops and ends. Characters may come and go—the Muse may take you off your outline, but if you have a pretty good idea where you want the book to end up, you'll get there by and by.

On the second or third draft—yes, before you send your book to an editor, you must edit and re-write your work. No book is written in its best form the first time around. Be careful with spelling and punctuation. If you don't know for certain you are correct in both, look up the word or the grammar structure and make sure you are correct.

📖 **You absolutely must find a professional editor and a proof reader—these are two different people with two different skill sets—to go through the book you think is finished.**

You'll discover there is much yet to be done to make the book saleable, marketable and accurate. Be open to criticism and suggestions to change the book to make it better. This is touchy and difficult for a lot of people. So often authors feel they have the only perspective that counts. Not so! Often everything from great ideas to humble corrections on obvious inconsistencies are impossible for the writer to find, simply because he is so close to the work. Let a little sunlight shine on your book from other people's eyes.

📖 **Of course, you can learn a lot from others.**

Identify your market before you start your book, know who your competition is, know your motivation for writing the book and read the kind of books you want to write.

By writing a book, the hundreds of thousands of writers who try to publish a book in any given year profess the same dreams as the American Idol wannabes. It takes courage to send a manuscript for evaluation. It takes persistence to keep sending it out after several rejections. It takes an ingrained belief in your book to self-publish and try to market it with all the cards stacked against you. But some do succeed if they have the money, time and dedication to do so.

To write well, it isn't enough to self-teach and self-edit. It is important to learn how to write from people who know how to write. And even more importantly, you need to hand over your writing to people who write and who have a discerning knowledge of writing to edit the work you produce.

Where does one go for this kind of attention, especially if one is working forty or more hours a week, has a family, is involved in the community and has precious few hours per week to devote to writing, much less the years it takes to learn how to write? Choices are numerous, even daunting.

Writing Coaches

Yvonne Perry (www.writersinthesky.com) began her writing service WRITE ON in 2003. "I began the company because I had a dream of being a writer and somehow making a living… so I did some pro-bono work, then I grew from a one-person freelance writing service to having now seven writers and we are growing at the seams…I work from my home, and because most of the writers are here in Nashville, we do get together to discuss the nuts and bolts of the business. But we do often use the phone and email to communicate.

"Writing coaches can act as ghostwriters, mentors, networkers and of course, they must be very good writers. They must be responsive to the client and work well with people.

"We have a variety of different types of writers, non-fiction, fiction, articles, press release, technical and business writers, and one writer who can write in both Spanish and English. We offer diversity and focus on various aspects of writing. Each project is matched to a writer on my team who can best work with the client or genre. We work together and often share details of the project with each other to better meet the needs of the client.

"A ghostwriter is someone who works invisibly behind the scenes, we may write a whole book or just an article for the author. We may serve as a coach or a mentor or we may polish or edit the manuscript to get it ready for a publisher. Ghostwriters don't receive credit because we're behind the scenes. That's why we're called 'ghosts.'"

📖 Continuing Education Courses, Writer's Workshops, Correspondence Writing Programs and Online Writing Courses.

In spite of the advantages of face-to-face instruction, not everyone can spare the time to go to a class. So, there are books, magazines, online and correspondence courses that can fill in the time gap. With the online and correspondence courses, you will work at your own pace and still get personalized instruction. You will not get the benefit of the free-flowing exchange of ideas and experience common to classes, conferences and workshops.

📖 **What you should get from your writing training, whether in a live class, a correspondence program or online course:**

📖 Clear how-to information, practice assignments and feedback

📖 A step-by-step syllabus or outline of the course

📖 Clearly described assignments that give you practical opportunity to write

📖 Teacher and peer feedback on your piece. You'll be called upon to give considered feedback of others' work as well.

📖 Thoughtful consideration of your piece and encouragement.

📖 Your work should be properly read, and evaluated with meaningful information on how to improve.

📖 Evaluation should begin with the positive comments and evolve to the more critical comments.

📖 Constructive criticism that focuses on clearly defined aspects of your work.

📖 Every writer can improve. No one is perfect. If you receive no critical information, you learn nothing.

📖 You should expect and require critical evaluation of your work that is helpful to your growth as a writer.

📖 If you are having trouble with point of view, for example, your evaluator needs to not only point out the problems, but provide helpful ways to fix the issues your writing presents.

Pat Diprima, founder of IN BLACK AND WHITE (www.writeinblackandwhite.com) says, "Writing is arguably the least visible and least appreciated of all the arts. You see people dancing across the stage. There are art galleries displaying the visual arts. Music is everywhere. But, we don't see too much of a writer writing, and I don't think the visibility of a book rack is all that exciting...I think writers need to get out there more, and because it is such a solitary process, they really don't get together the way they should."

Most beginning workshops or classes should teach at least these five skills:

📖 How to show rather than tell.
📖 How to use the five senses or even the sixth.
📖 How to grab your reader with a great story opening.
📖 How interesting characters, or in nonfiction interesting people, maintain reader attention.
📖 How to get the big picture on plot, by delineating circular plots, character-driven, action driven plots etc. in clear terms with examples.

However, as Ms. DiPrima points out, "The workshop won't do the writing itself. A lot of writers have very unrealistic expectations. They think they can...just sit down and dash off something. But writing is an art...that takes a lot of hard work and discipline more than anything else."

The live class or workshops can deal with more difficult problems in a more personal way. For example, here is what Ms. DiPrima says about writer's block: "Writer's block is usually a fear, their fear that they won't succeed, or it's a fear that they have succeeded and now can they live up to it."

📖 What about books and Magazines for "How-to write" Information?

In the multiplicity of printed writing resources, the best known are offered by Writer's Digest Books and Magazine at www.writersdigest.com

Writer's Digest Books is has been a publisher of books for writers for more than 75 years—starting in 1921 with publication of Writer's Market—the resource for writers, from reference information to sources for getting published to techniques for perfecting your craft: www.WritersMarket.com

📖 Correspondence and Online Courses are an option for busy writers.

📖 Writer's Digest

Provided by Writer's Digest to brush up on the basics, start writing poetry or have a particular problem with your novel, Writers Online Workshops offers forty-three workshops from the publisher of Writer's Digest taught by forty-nine professional writers. www.writersonlineworkshops.com

📖 Long Ridge Writing Project

Long Ridge Writers Group offers a program that has, for 30 years, taught thousands of aspiring writers how to find their own writing niche—and how to break into print.

One-on-one personalized instruction from a faculty of professional writers and experienced editors. College Credits are available for their program. Instruction is available everywhere via the traditional home study method—with lessons exchanged through the mail or via the Internet. www.longridgewritersgroup.com/

Community Colleges and Universities

Community colleges are two year post-secondary institutions that offer certificate programs, Associate of Arts degree, Associate of Sciences degrees, plus many other programs. According to latest statistics from the American Association of Community Colleges (AACC), http://www.aacc.nche.edu/ there are 1,166 community colleges in the United States.

The University of Texas at Austin lists all the community colleges in the United State by state www.utexas.edu/world/comcol/state/

If you are looking for a degree level course in writing, the most comprehensive online listing is offered at American Universities at http://www.clas.ufl.edu/au/

A list of international universities is available at http://www.findaschool.org/.

A list of Canadian universities is available at http://www.uwaterloo.ca/canu/

Shaw Guides

The Guide to Writers Conferences & Workshops is the most comprehensive listing of local, national and international conferences and workshops where writers of every stripe can find colleagues, learn the newest techniques and practice the craft of writing. Listings at http://writing.shawguides.com/

Writing Groups

Not everyone can go back to college, or hire a writing coach or afford a far-flung workshop or conference. Some of the best alternate choices reside quietly in the libraries and community colleges across the country. The writing groups that evolve to help writers learn and grow can provide excellent training and feedback. While some are geared toward 'all genre welcome' standards, others are particular to poetry, short story, novels, and non-fiction, and within those broad categories, one can find particular interests, such as mystery, sci-fi, romance, children's books and so on. The National Association of Women Writers (www.naww.com) is a great place for women writers to connect.

I asked Colleen Kappler, founder of the Kenosha Writer's Group, in Kenosha, Wisconsin www.prosenest.com to describe a typical writer in her writing group.

"We have everyone from twenty year olds to eighty year olds. We have people who write fiction, who write horror, who are working on their memoirs, books, articles and short stories, and some are working towards creating publishable pieces, and others are there because they love writing and the writing group keeps them committed to writing every month…a lot of people are not really to a point where they want to attempt publishing it…some have been doing this a long time and they've become really good at the re-writing, which I think is the crucial part of writing."

We also discussed some of the benefits of being part of a writing group. Colleen pointed out that, "It is an invaluable experience to be able to share your work with a group that is actually a subgroup of your readers, and hear what your readers are responding to in your work, what they are understanding or not understanding [helps] you improve your writing."

As the conversation turned toward critique, I asked her to describe how she handles this touchy requirement of a good writer's group. "We work a lot on not defending or explaining your writing because…[it is important] to step back and listen to everyone around the table critique…if people don't understand something, you're not going to be there when it's published to explain it to people, so explaining it across the table isn't going to work. Critiques are difficult because people can become defensive."

I also talked with Alison Wilmes, Program Director at the Grayslake Public Library in Grayslake, Illinois, about how their writers groups benefit aspiring authors.

"They are places of encouragement and support, certainly. So, you can get critiques from fellow members, and you get to analyze their work to see what works and what do other people think is working for them, and then take that information and use it with your own work…And, a lot of time with our writing groups, we bring in authors to talk with the writers about the writing process, publishing, legal aspects related to copyright law, so there is a lot of information you get in addition to learning how to be a good writer. A lot of people do belong to multiple groups and gain from the variety they get in the different groups."

📖 EDITORS

Kathleen Kearney is a freelance editor, who has edited a number of our titles. She has given clear descriptions of what editing is and what it might cost.

Developmental editing is where you really have to help the author re-organize the work and consider plot and character issues.

"[The editor] reads the whole work several times, to get the whole gist of the plot, to figure out what the author is trying to say and what the novel is about, because the author thinks [the plot] is going somewhere where it is not necessarily going…that we have a plot with an introduction, a climax and a conclusion and all the details we need to understand what the author is trying to get across.

"The editor deals with character issues of flat, non-dynamic characters who don't add anything to the plot or who don't really fit into the plot. The author has the whole story in his head, but the reader or editor doesn't see the same view. This is where the author learns from his editor."

Point of view editing is where the editor helps the author keep the point of view consistent. "In one manuscript I was editing most recently, each chapter had a different point of view, meaning jumping from the third person narrator back to the first person character. Point of view editing needs to make sure the author keeps the point of view consistent."

Grammatical and syntactical issues the editor has to "…distinguish the use of poor grammar in dialog for character from the use of poor grammar in the entire book. The cowboy in a story is likely going to say "ain't," but if you're saying that within your narration, that is probably not an okay word to use. Also we have to make sure that the syntax and form of the sentences are correct...spell and grammar check is often very wrong. People often think that as long as they run a spell check or a grammar check in Microsoft Word that they are in the clear. You do need a human to read your manuscript...the computer can't think, it just processes."

What editing is NOT—it is not proofreading for typos, for example, although sometimes it's hard to resist making corrections.

Kathleen clarifies editing this way: "It is not a lot of things that people stereotypically think that it is. It is not my going through a manuscript seeing if the author has put in capital letters. Content editing is what an editor does, as opposed to correcting details as a proof reader does."

Pricing—by word, by page, by job—it is often hard to spend money for fear of being bilked or getting a bad edit.

Kathleen points out that, "The editor should see the work to determine the scope of the project. An editor should take into consideration life situations when pricing a job. The editor should be willing to discuss the project first hand with the author to be sure what the editor is being asked to do."

When I asked her to give a guideline about pricing, she replied, "Pricing a job at $.01 per word is pretty standard among freelance editors. But, if a manuscript is 200,000 words, the author may balk at a bill of $2000, so I will discount the job."

Pricing varies greatly and is most often determined on a per word basis. But, there are editors who charge by the page or by the job. Here is a broad guideline for all three pricing schedules:

Per Word: If your manuscript is 75,000 words and the editor is charging $.01 (which is pretty standard among freelance editors) to $.05 per word, your cost is going to be $750 to $3750 for the editing job.

Per Page: If your manuscript is 300 pages, and the editor is charging $1 to $3 per page, your cost is going to be $300 to $900 for the job.

Per Job: This is the most negotiable. Generally, you can expect a charge of $350 to $500 for the job approach. **A word of caution:** If the editor is charging thousands of dollars for the job, do not do business with that firm. We had an author whose work came back in a document format that was foreign and unusable. The author had to take it to a software specialist to try to salvage his mansucript. The errors were still in the work, and he had to hire another editor to do the job again.

PUNCTUATION and GRAMMAR

Authors make basic punctuation errors all the time. The following items represent the most common mistakes writers make. If they appear in your manuscript, you should correct them prior to submission. This is a time consuming task, which if you do it yourself, you will save an enormous amount of money. If your publisher has to do this, he will charge for the work. If you pay a copyeditor and/or a proofreader, make sure you get what you pay for. Either way, you need to know the punctuation conventions of writing. If you don't, buy *THE*

ELEMENTS OF STYLE by William Strunk. This book has set the style and grammar standard for decades.

📖 📖 📖

📖 **Be sure to correct your manuscript before submission to an agent or a publisher.**

📖 **PARAGRAPH SPACING and FORMAT:**
📖 Format your paragraphs to be JUSTIFIED only.
📖 Every Paragraph needs to be indented .35"
📖 Every time someone speaks, that's a new paragraph.
📖 There should be no additional space between paragraphs.
📖 There should be ONE space after a period, not two spaces.

📖 **COMMAS, PERIODS, QUESTION MARKS, EXCLAMATION POINTS, SEMICOLONS AND COLONS AND QUOTATION MARKS:**
📖 Commas and periods occur immediately after a word. There should be no space between a word and the punctuation.
📖 Commas, periods, question marks and exclamation points ALWAYS occur INSIDE quotation marks, even quotation marks that are not part of a character's speech:
She gave him an apple, the "forbidden fruit."
📖 Each punctuation mark that ends a sentence is unique and is not used in conjunction with any other (except for quotation marks). This means you may not use a comma after a question mark (?,) for example, or a comma and a period (,.) or any other combination.

📖 Semicolons connect two longer sentences that are related in topic and are not used to create lists.
📖 Colons are often used before a list.
📖 Use commas to list several items if necessary, not semicolons.
📖 Never repeat exclamation points and question marks to show emphasis. Let your choice of words do that.
📖 When a person is speaking and quoting someone else, use the following convention:
"I heard Jack say 'Shut up!' just before the sound of the gunshot."

📖 ELLIPSIS AND EM DASHES:

📖 In spoken passages, the ellipsis (...) means someone has purposely omitted saying something and should be used very sparingly. Do not use it to show someone's voice has faded away. Use description to do that.
📖 In the descriptive paragraph the ellipsis is used to show a pause in the action. Do not over use this, as it becomes aggravating to the reader.
📖 The Em dash (—) is a relative of the parentheses, and is used to add a qualifying thought or a minor clarification of the topic.
📖 The parentheses () is used to set off added information specific to the topic.

📖 ITALICS FOR FOREIGN LANGUAGES AND THOUGHTS:

📖 Consistency is very important.

📖 If you use italics for foreign languages, do not use quotation marks, unless the character actually speaks the foreign language and you are translating a foreign language to English in the body of your manuscript. Either way, whether spoken or not, it is best to use italics for the foreign language, and set the English translation off with parentheses. Example:

📖 Jacques said, "*Elle est extremement belle.*" (She is very beautiful.)

📖 *Le ciel était vert avant l'orage.* (The sky was green before the storm.)

📖 If the character's thought is contained in a spoken passage, italics help differentiate what is verbal from what is non-verbal.

Example:
"I don't like your tone of voice. *Actually, I don't like you.* I think you'd better step out of the room," Mr. Smithfield said to the apprentice.

📖 SPELLING, GRAMMAR AND COMPUTER SPELL CHECK/GRAMMAR FUNCTIONS:

When your computer tells you a word is spelled right, it may be wrong. Here are a few of the commonly missed spellings:

- 📖 Too, to, two
- 📖 Through, threw
- 📖 There, their
- 📖 Here, hear
- 📖 Who's, whose

There are many, many times when the computer doesn't distinguish between spellings for the sense of the word. You need to know.

Most grammar functions would correct this statement as follows or miss it altogether:

More times than not, the grammar function on computers is wrong.

More times than not, the grammar function on computers are wrong. *(Incorrect, because 'computers' is not the subject of the verb, it is the object of the preposition)*

More times than not, the grammar function on computers is wrong. *(Correct, because 'grammar function' is the singular subject of the verb to be, but the computer grammar function didn't know that.)*

📖 📖 📖

📖 ONLINE RESOURCES:

📖 The Blue Book of Grammar and Punctuation
http://www.grammarbook.com/

Do you need this book? Try one of the Interactive Tests to find out. Receive your scores and the correct answers instantly.

📖 Grammar, Punctuation, and Spelling / Purdue University Online Writing Lab.
http://owl.english.purdue.edu/handouts/grammar/

This extremely comprehensive site includes printer friendly versions and Adobe PDF versions of all of the grammar handouts available and also provides exercises and answers.

The Grammar section includes Adjectives and adverbs, Nouns, Prepositions, Pronouns, Sentence structure, Verbs, Tense Consistency

The Punctuation section includes Apostrophes and Quotation Marks, Commas, Sentence Fragments, Spelling: accept/except, Spelling: i/e rules.

📖 Punctuation Made Simple

http://lilt.ilstu.edu/golson/punctuation/intro.html

Written to help de-mystify the details of punctuation, this resource covers the most commonly used, but not all punctuation and grammar conventions with the intent of providing a more generalized sense of how and why punctuation works. This site is for good writers who have a command of punctuation and grammar, but who need more understanding of the origins and flexibility of both.

Getting the details of your book right is a lengthy, sometimes costly process which is essential to the ultimate success of the book. Well-written books have a better chance at the gold ring in publishing. But, as with all the arts, there are many, many more talented, well-trained writers who remain unknown and often unpublished than there are published, well-known writers. Often, the author's ability to market surpasses the author's ability to write. Best sellers are not always the best written books. However, there is also always room on the shelves for another book that meets the public's demand for good, even great writing. New books will come and go. Some will remain to become classics. Some start out slow and grow, while others hit the market hard and fast and then fade into oblivion. But, it is a certainty that if the book is properly written, edited, produced and published, it will find its market, however large or small that market may be.

Make a list of the writing resources and assistance you will need to write your book:

I will write _____ hours every day.

I need to research these items: _____
_____
_____
_____
_____
_____
_____

I will make an outline ____Yes ____No

I need an editor ____Yes

I need a writing coach ____Yes ____No

I should look into these options:

_____Continuing Education Courses
_____Writer's Workshops
_____Correspondence Writing Programs
_____Online Writing Courses
_____Library Writing Groups

📖 RATE YOURSELF (Be honest here) T = true F = false
Informative answers are available at the back of the book.

___I am really good at grammar. I got all A's in school.

___I am really good at spelling. I got all A's in school.

___I read all the time and find mistakes others have made.

___I know the difference between prepositions and interrogatives. Some common prepositions are: _____The interrogatives are: ____, ____, ____, ____, ____

___I know adverbs modify verbs.

___I know adjectives modify nouns.

___I know subject pronouns are:

___, ___, ___, ___, ___, ___, ___

___I know the possessive pronouns are:

___, ___, ___, ___, ___, ___, ___, ___, ___, ___, ___, ___

___I know what the pluperfect tense is. Example sentence:_____

_____

___I know how to use the conditional tense accurately with other tenses. Examples sentences:_____

_____

_____

_____

___I know what the Past Conditional Tense is. Example sentence:_____

_____

___I know there are two kinds of present tense. They are the _____ and the _____

___ I know there are two kinds of past tense. They are
the_____ and the _____

___ I know how to use the future tense. Example sentence:_____
_____

___ I know what the future anterior tense is and when to use it. Example sentence:_____
_____

___ I know what the passive voice is: Example sentence_____
_____

___ I know what the active voice is: Example sentence_____
_____

___ I know the articles. They are: ___, ___, ___.

___ I know what the demostrative articles are:
_____, _____, _____, _____

___ I know what a gerund is. Example sentence: _____
_____

This simple quiz will give you a sense of what you know and do not know. Get help if you are unsure of anything in the statements above or could not give an example sentence.

CHAPTER 5

Can you tell a book by its cover?

It is with words as with sunbeams.
The more they are condensed, the deeper they burn.
—Robert Southey, 1774-1843

You've gone to the long and arduous task of writing your book. You have prepared your marketing plan. You have your Web site, your blog and your newsletter email list. Your publisher has prepared the layout and design of your book and refuses to use your cover design. You just love the Old English alphabet, and yellow is your favorite color. You title is witty, though it is ten words long and somewhat obscure. What do you care? It will intrigue the prospective buyer, or so you think. Well, think again.

The cover and the spine of the book are what will make the buyer pick your book from all the others. The eye rests for about three to five seconds, even less according to some, on the cover before moving on. If your publisher is arguing with you over the design of the cover, you had better listen.

Here is a great exercise I heard from Jan Nathan during an interview where we covered many topics.

"I suggest authors and publishers go out to a bookstore and walk the shelves and look at the books to see what titles leap out at you... HEALTHY AGING. Boy, does that tell me what that book is about. I can read it and see it easily. What are the titles, colors and what leaps out at you and how does it leap out at you. So many times the title should be the subtitle. Short and to the point....Can you say briefly what your book is about and make the title five words or less and still say what the book is about? The back cover has a blurb that leads them inside the book, and if you can get them to do that, they will probably buy it."

📖 COVERS

First, the cover must be in tune with the content. I believe the mystery thriller and the book on choosing surrogacy over adoption require completely different approaches. I agree that the title should be legible from a distance of six feet. And, the author's name should be prominent. The hints to the content can be part of the design, and design should in some way reflect the content. Children's books should convey the sense of the story, and in no uncertain terms, hinting at content doesn't work with kids.

On every cover for our authors, we have included these elements, whether fiction, non-fiction or children's books

📖 Titles in large, easily readable type
📖 Author's name in large, easily readable type
📖 Colorful imagery that hints at or tells what's inside, sets a mood, reflects a story line
📖 Subtitles that reveal more---always for non-fiction, children's and sometimes for fiction
📖 Back cover copy that expands on the subtitles and/or teases the story content to entice readers to open the book

📖 Quotes from reviews and award logos when possible
📖 The author's head shot, price, and genre

Ken Sturgis, past president of PMA provides a comprehensive list of what covers should contain. Here are the most relevant points:

📖 "Books are bought on impulse more often than not.

📖 The best advertising for a book is its cover. No sale is made if, in a second or two, nothing on the cover attracts interest.

📖 There is no one right or wrong way to design a cover.

📖 But you should understand that some buyers may pass on a nonfiction title if its cover design strikes them as odd, vague, or ambiguous, and some certainly will hesitate about buying nonfiction if they cannot infer the content from elements of the cover.

📖 Try to make the cover answer the question, "What is this book?" And remember that a beautiful, dazzling cover is not necessarily the right cover if all elements are not working together. Be careful of fancy fonts, too. They might look good, but can they be read from a distance?

In my little corner of the publishing universe, a successful cover is a happy marriage of art and commerce."

📖 TITLES

Susan Kendrick of Write To Your Market, Inc. seven great tips for making the title unforgettable.

"1. **Use a twist on a familiar phrase.** Take This Job and Love It is a great example. Unfortunately, because book titles cannot be copyrighted, a Take This Job title appears on several different books.

2. **Use a vivid image to grab people on some gut level.** But make sure your subtitle instantly clarifies what your book is about and what it does for the reader. The subtitle of Swim with the Sharks is: Outsell, Outmanage, Outmotivate, and Outnegotiate Your Competition—four premium benefits for the business market.

3. **Use four-letter words (OK, even five).** New York Times bestsellers *Take Back Your Life* and *Stand Up for Your Life* by Cheryl Richardson show how simple, everyday words can be turned into powerful titles. Book titles are a one-on-one conversation with your reader, and you also want to make an impact on reviewers, distributors, bookstores, and your industry peers.

4. **Look to the book itself.** This is one of the most overlooked sources of great titles. Often a great chapter title quickly translates into a powerful book title.

5. **Choose clarity over cleverness.** If in doubt, simply say exactly what the book is. Keep in mind that a nonfiction book will ideally become a great lead generator for the author, the author's services, and any related products. Make sure the title reflects the author's credibility.

6. **Use search engines.** To find strong key words for a title, test possibilities at www.overture.com under "Visit the Resource Center" and then "Key Word Selector Tool." The goal here is to tie into what people are searching for online.

7. **Use a number to attract attention.** Look what *The Seven Habits of Highly Effective People* has done for Stephen Covey. A number provides a

great way to give readers a tangible sense of the benefits they will receive and the ease with which they can use your book to get results."

📖 There is No Right or Wrong Way to Design a Cover

Well, I agree and I disagree. I agree to the extent that no one design concept has the absolute and definitive edge over all other design concepts. I agree that those who approach cover design as gallery art are entirely missing the point of the job a cover has to do—attract the eye in seconds.

I disagree to the extent that many authors who come to us with their own ideas of what their cover should be, often are unaware of what I will call the technical components of a cover's design. Some want too much imagery, others want too little. Some think a font choice is unimportant and want the frilliest font in the list. While others want un-imaginative layout, with images floating all over the cover with no connection. It becomes a clear challenge to tactfully suggest an illustrator take over the artwork, or to prepare a cover concept which the author can appreciate more than his own idea.

And cover design is in the eye of the beholder, as is all art, actually. What one person likes, another may not like. What attracts one reader, may not attract another. It is virtually impossible to design a cover that will please all the people all the time. So, the publisher's job is to make certain that whether the cover is designed by a paid illustrator, graphic designer, or done in house, the cover attractively represents the content of the book.

📖 Internet Viewing

Book covers must be visible on the computer screen and the visibility of the cover from online bookstores to the publisher's own bookstore is crucial. Just 10% of all books are sold online according to American Bookseller's Association, but that is due to rise. Small publishers sell books to the tune of $11 billion a year, from their own Web sites as well as in stores. So it is important to consider the look of the book in its thumbnail presentation on the web. Some sites, Amazon among them, offer a larger view of the cover. This helps. We have used several design approaches depending on the content of the book: Some examples are:

📖 Non-fiction

Dying to be Young—Surviving Botulism, A True Story: The full face of the woman, with eyes closed, and the syrigne pointing toward her smile line says it all. Simple, powerful, and revealing the topic of the book.

America's Fighting Force: intense black and green colors. Elongated Photos of night goggle views of military hardware, lights pictures of soldiers being humorous, review quotes.

Surrogacy was the Way: mother and children walking hand in hand on a leaf-strewn path—author and her children —soft colors for the background pulled from the photo. Lots of quotes in review of the work.

📖 Historical Fiction

And the Sea Shall Hide Them: moonlit view of a schooner (central to the theme of the story) and red and silver script font (reference to the bloody murder, moonlight), faces of the real people set in ovals appearing to be "shining" down on the scene. Review content and short tease.

Black River Crossing: Photo of actual Black River, the setting for the story, rocky section with blue sky and full verdant green landscape. Gives impression of wild flowing water—like the story. Bright Red Bold lettering in vivid contrast to the natural background image.

The House of Triblinkus: Linedrawing/colorwash artwork depicting the murder that is central to the tale. Very Edgar Allen Poe. Chilling.

📖 Thriller

The Resort: Black cover with red exotic flower, a symbol of the main character and grows only in the South Pacific where this fast paced tale takes place. Red lettering that makes titles and author name easy to read and works well with the flower.

The Fugitive Hour: The Catalina plane is integral to the plot of this adventurous tale, so to put it on the cover, in black and white to emphasize that the story takes place in the past, before color television, is a perfect lead-in to the tale itself.

Sidetracks: A box image of a painting of two paths diverging in a forest hints at the main theme of this mystery: that we could have taken a different path in life. How would things have turned out if you had done something differently at a particularly crucial moment?

📖 Children's

The Punctuation Pals Series: bright colors, child friendly illustration that clearly depicts the content of the story where the Pals Go to School, Go to a Baseball park, Go Snow Skiing, Go to the Moon and Go to the Beach.

Inside Our Fridge: Line drawing from the title poem set in whimsical turquoise border with simple, hand lettering font. Fun and sassy.

Arthur, the Christmas Elf: The elf himself, his trusty reindeer, familiar, yet new, painted in acrylics and bold colors. Appealing and friendly faces that draw you into the book.

I could go on and on. Others might have done these covers differently, but they work well on the book and on the Web sites. They are highly visible and give the reader a sense of the content. The quotes from reviews and awards logos are a plus.

📖 THE SPINE

Designing the spine is just about the hardest part of the book designer's job. This is the only view that most books get to present to the world. Face out placement on bookstore shelves is unlikely for most books. Libraries show only the spines of most books as well. So, the half to one inch wide space must grab the eye, it must leap out from the shelf in some way that the other books do not.

Certainly a short, clear title is key. Many publishers have begun to stack the words vertically rather than forcing the browsing customer to twist his head sideways to read the title. Often, only the last name of the author is visible. And the font is simple and bold, and the color is bright.

Often, the publisher's logo also appears on the spine. It may be placed at the top, or the bottom of the spine. This is one way publisher's advertise their companies. It is customary and proper.

Kathi Dunn, whose Web site is www.dunn-design.com , explains the details of creating a great book spine in her PMA Independent article *"Show Me Some Spine! How to Create Book Spines that Grab Readers,"*

"...When constructing the spine in your book-cover layout, think about how the cover will be printed. A perfect-bound, softcover book has distinct, clean edges where the spine meets the front and back covers. But a case-bound book's dust jacket has smooth, curved, less distinct edges forming the spine, which means that visual elements can wrap from the spine onto the front cover and weaken its impact. To create a smooth visual transition on a dust jacket, it is often wise to extend visual elements intentionally from the front cover onto the spine and back cover."

I agree with Kathi on this, but it also works on certain kinds of perfect-bound covers. When there is a bold, wide stripe highlighting the front title, or a picture that is not bounded by a rectangle border, these images can wrap to the back to carry the look all the way around the book. I often will put the shortest part of the title, three to five words, on the spine, stacked vertically for easy reading, our logo at the bottom.

On William Jackson's historical fiction novel, *And the Sea Shall Hide Them*, the cover image on this perfect-bound book wraps around to the back cover and fades into white.

Zara Griswold's book, *Surrogacy Was the Way*, we reflected the front cover image on the back cover, with the reflecting edges coming together on the spine. We then placed a 60% transparent overlay on the back image to allow for easy reading of the back cover copy.

Whatever you do about the design of your cover, let go of your preconceptions and let your publisher advise you. If you are self-publishing, pay someone to design your cover. It will be the best investment in your book's success that you can make.

📖REVEIW

Think about your book's cover here. You can change your ideas, but it is a good thing to try out a few concepts before you talk WI th your designer. Practice here.

Use a twist on a familiar phrase. _____

Use a vivid image to grab people on some gut level. _____

Use four-letter words (OK, even five). _____

Look to the book itself. _____

Choose clarity over cleverness. _____

Use search engines. _____

Use a number to attract attention. _____

Your SHORT TITLE: _____
Your SUBTITLE: _____

Cover Image ideas: Remember to reflect the main theme of your book:
1. _____
2. _____
3. _____
4. _____
5. _____

SPINE
Vertical Lettering _____   Traditional lettering _____

CHAPTER 6

How hard is it to sell a book?

I couldn't wait for success...so I went ahead without it.
—Jonathan Winters, 1925-

Authors are true believers. They believe in the face of impossible odds. Somewhere inside, they know their book is the next bestseller. It is of no concern to them that there are already millions of books in the marketplace. Nor does it faze them there are roughly 55,000 publishers in the United State alone who publish 200,000 plus books every year. That's more than 500 books a day. And, never mind that only 1,200 books, novels, short stories, and plays have been made into motion pictures as feature-length films in the United States, in English, since 1980. Do the math. Twenty-seven years divided into 1,200 books produces 44 books made into movies per year. Divide that by 200,000 and you get .022% of all books per year ever become films. Theirs is going to be the next blockbuster. Move over J.K. Rowling, and R.R. Tolkien. Yours are not the only epic series that are worthy.

"Ah, hah!" you say. "Your math is inaccurate. Fewer books were published in 1980 than in 2006."

"Yes," I reply. "But even if we used 100,000 books per year, the numbers would still come to less than one one-hundredth of a percent. Not many," I'd say.

And so it is. But, authors are true believers. And so, I thought it would be interesting to quote authors who have faced the crush of competition with their books and who have talked about how they sell their books.

Shirley Cheng, The Revelation of a Star's Endless Shine:
"I maintain my own Web site, www.shirleycheng.com and www.dancewithyourheart.com . I post press releases whenever I have an event, I'm scheduling booksignings at local bookstores, I have been on seventeen radio shows, I join newsletters and discussion groups, and I have six basic marketing strategies on my email signature."

Chuck McCann, Short, Shorter and Shorter Stories:
"I carry my books in the car all the time, because almost anywhere you go today, people are waiting, and I ask them if they'd like to have a book to read while they're waiting. I managed to get into a group that was auditioning as guest speakers, and I told some of the stories. And on our river cruise in Europe, when the travelers put on a little show on the cruise, I told some of the stories and people bought the book from me. I send out flyers to libraries to get scheduled as a speaker. I put the cover of the book on the front and back of the tee shirt I wear, and carry my business card to hand out as people ask about the book."

Michael Stadther: A Treasure Trove and The Secrets of the Alchemist Dar:
"I write event books where a treasure hunt for a million dollars in jewels draws readers into the story to find the gold tokens and redeem them for the jewels. Families would work

together to try to solve the mystery, and the books fell apart after being read a thousand times, so we published a spiral bound version. I tied the jewels into the story, I had to contact jewelers to create the prizes, and scatter them all over the world myself. Fourteen tokens were found by fourteen groups of people from all walks of life, children, parents, grad students and others. I put additional clues on the Web site, and two remain unsolved, which for the foreseeable future they will remain unsolved."

The Three P'S and I Don't Mean Vegetables

When I was teaching high school French, as the years passed, I noticed that those students who did the best were those who used what I have come to call the three P's. Planning, Practice and Persistence. Later in my career in the public high school realm, I was teaching in an "at risk" high school with an over-crowded population of "at risk" students, many of whom were clinging to their school lives by a thread. They didn't know how to study. No one had taught them how to organize anything. They were at a loss as to how to plan ahead, prepare for exams, see into their futures for a glimpse of who they wanted to be when they grew up. Typically, these students were more interested the social aspects of school than they were in the academic pursuits that could help them grow beyond the borders of their "at risk" world. Many of them were teetering on the brink of self-destruction because of the temptations of drugs, sex, and a culture of helplessness. They were not expected to succeed, and so they didn't try to learn how succeed.

"So what?" you say. "What does this have to do with my being a writer trying to sell my books?" Well, quite a lot, actually. First-time authors are a lot like my at risk students:

insecure, distracted, delusional, uninformed, without skills to prepare for what's ahead of them.

Let's take the first P and apply it to the world of writing, books and publishing.

📖 PLANNING

The planning process applies to the creation of the book and to the selling of the book.

📖 Creation Planning

For fiction, the plot, characters and theme of the story don't (or shouldn't) just happen. The author plans the overview of the action, the character's personalities, the impact of events, the reason for the story in the first place. Even if the author doesn't design a detailed outline for his book, he should work out the flow of his book on paper before he begins writing. Some will do this in reverse, write the book and then organize it, making changes to accommodate the re-organization. But, the planning is the skeleton for the story, and wherever the creative Muse takes it, at least there is a first plan.

For non-fiction, in many ways these books are easier to write. There is an over-riding goal to inform, convince, sell or inspire—or a combination of all these factors—to the planning stage. Outlines are common for non-fiction books. This doesn't mean changes don't happen. They do. But the book should have a clear step-by-step organization to it. The broad outline helps shape the beauty of the book, in much the same way the bone structure shapes the silhouette of the high-fashion model.

📖 Marketing Planning

All too often, this part of the process of a book's life is minimized or over-looked altogether.

"When does the marketing begin?" you ask.

Before the book is completed. At the very least, while the book is in the hands of the publisher for layout and design, after sending the manuscript in for its first copyright registration (www.loc.gov form TX, short form) the author needs to be sending manuscripts to online reviewers and notable people who can provide endorsements for use on the cover of the book, and selected local media, in preparation for the galley and the book's release—usually about 3 to 5 months after the galley is out.

Then with the galley, the author should be setting up booksignings, entering tradeshows and awards programs, getting on radio shows, local TV newscasts, sending the galley to mainstream reviewers, and building a press kit from the results of his efforts.

At the release of the book, the author should be actually doing the events he has set up for his book.

"That a lot of work! How does a single author manage all that?" you ask.

One step at a time from the clear, line item outline. The time and effort is considerable, and that is why there are people who are publicity experts who can help in the process. It costs money, sometimes a lot of money, and there is no guarantee that the publicity generated will actually sell the book. But, creating a buzz is essential. To do nothing is to gain nothing.

📖 PRACTICE

Just like learning a musical instrument, or memorizing a poem, or preparing a speech, writing and marketing take practice. Make this your motto, it's old but true: "If at first you don't succeed, try, try again." Any author trying to sell his book is going to try many kinds of exposure that don't work. Also, she will try things that do work. Those are the ones to practice. They are the ones to expand upon, to modify, to re-create a gain and again. Thinking outside the book is an essential ingredient to the practice of marketing a book successfully. Even when writing the book, knowing there is something in the story or the information it contains that will intrigue the public and consciously putting that "something" into your book take practice.

📖 PERSISTENCE

This is the hardest aspect of writing and marketing a book. Keeping the focus on your task, repeating the process of exposing the book again and again, never giving up on the book itself takes a strong constitution. It takes *BELIEF*. Belief in the book, in yourself, and in the process of trial and error as realized in the serendipity of finding the best market for your book and reaching it. Some of this is planned. Some of this is practiced. But, *most* of this is persistence driven.

Consider this idea quoted from Samuel Butler:

"The oldest books are still only just out to those who have not read them."
—Samuel Butler

His satirical novel Erewhon appeared anonymously in 1872, causing some speculation as to the identity of the author. When Butler revealed himself as the author, some expressed disappointment that none of the more famous personages speculated about had written it. Erewhon made Butler a well-known figure, and he wrote a number of other books, including a not so successful sequel, Erewhon Revisited. His semi-autobiographical novel The Way of All Flesh did not appear in print until after his death in 1902, as he considered its tone of attack on Victorian hypocrisy too contentious.

Jan Nathan, Director of PMA puts getting a book to sell this way.

"Many PMA members have books that have sold 200, 300, 400 thousand but not in the first couple of years. Maybe it takes 10 years, maybe it takes 8 years. So, having these books that can reach those numbers, they are long term reachable. We are the slow and steady and will eventually finish the race."

"If your book has been published, and you have done all the things you can possibly do to make it successful, and it doesn't reach whatever goal you have set for it, what then?" you ask.

The Answer Is: Never, Ever Quit.

Keep re-inventing your marketing approach. Use Ezine articles, Blogs, and Podcasts to spread the word. Go to the stores and shops that fit your niche both online and locally to get you book on the shelves. Get out of your comfort zone and promote, again and again. Send out press releases every time you do anything notable with you book. Talk to people everywhere you can think of about your book. Give presentations in schools and libraries. Keep going to tradeshows. Keep your book visible. In the end, there is a lot of luck involved too. But, if you give up, it's all over.

BOOKSTORES, LIBRARIES and Alternative Markets

Bookstores

The very name seems to answer the question, "Where do I sell my book?" Every author dreams of the day his book is sitting face out on the shelves with customers struggling with each other to grab the last copy. But in reality, bookstores are very hard to get into, and if you do, the percentages you have to pay the distributor to promote the book to the stores takes 60 or 65 percent of the retail price right off the top. Then you take away the print cost, and what is left goes to the publisher and the author. However, then there are the returns, those books that were unsold or damaged in transit. Those are all charged back against whatever the book originally earned. Sometimes these deductions mean there is very little left over.

Libraries

There are over ten thousand libraries in the United States, and they often buy books that the bookstores will not buy. It is a huge market, though not as glamorous as the bookstore mystique, and it does require hardbound books, for the most part. There are often rotating kiosks of mass market paperbacks near the fiction section of the library, but those rotate out as they fall apart, and many are donated items.

📖 Alternative markets

This is where the small publisher and their authors can do very well. No huge discounts to distributors to reduce the profits. No returns and get paid in thirty days. Creative marketing is limited only by the imagination.

Jan Nathan of Publisher's marketing Association gives a couple of great examples of how this is done.

"We have a publisher member of PMA who…had a book called "1001 Ways to be Romantic" and thought it would be hard to place it a general bookstore. So, he went into Victoria's Secret, told them "Place my book on the countertops and I'll turn your countertops into dollars for you." He sells thousands and thousands of books every year at Christmas and Valentine's Day.

"Catalogues like Quality Paperbacks often lead your book into the bookstores because the catalogue will create the demand. One of our members went to Kellogg's and sold their guide to the historic bed and breakfast inns around the country as a premium on the cereal box. Just because a book hasn't been sold in a particular place, doesn't mean it won't be."

Corporations, hospitals, healthclubs, all sorts of specialty shops, developing bookclubs, meet the author fanclubs and internet webinars or teleseminars are great ways to sell books. The creative author and publisher can develop many new ways to market books by thinking beyond the bookstore.

📖 AMAZON BestSeller List

This is not as inaccessible as you may think. Depending on how many authors are doing an Amazon Splash (or Blast) on any given day, it is possible to get a rating of "best seller" by teaming up all your contacts and all their contacts to purchase your book all on the same day. The Best Seller status is given to books that sell five hundred to a thousand books or more on one day.

This requries planning, with plenty of time ahead to make sure your book is easily ordered on Amazon. Once that is established, the next steps are the following:

📖 Prepare your Splash (or Blast) email campaign

Write an introductory letter, specially targeting your various interested contacts.

📖 Gather together as many give away gifts from other people as you can.

These gifts can be eBooks, Teleseminars, and hour of specialized coaching, how-to information, and whatever else you can find to easily provide as a download from your Web site, which you will list liberally in your email campaign letter. Try to make your total value significant, $500 or more to better entice people to purchase your book on the particular day.

📖 Send your first announcement email about two weeks days before the target day.

Ask everyone to send your announcement to all those on their email lists. This requires plenty of pre-Splash asking, cajoling and the like. But, the more of your contacts you can talk with to pump up their enthusiasm for your event, the better.

📖 Send a followup reminder the day before the Splash date.

And send a reminder on the day of the Splash date.

📖 **It is even more helpful to plan some media event, such as a radio and/or television interview about your book for the day of your Splash.**

Then you can announce it to the listening or viewing audience as well.

📖 **Amazon typically discounts all books 30% or more.**

The giveaways are such a great bonus, it can truly be of value for your customers to get the $500 or more gifts as well. Also, discount your book on your Web site.

📖 **Continue to give the gifts** from your Web site or blog after the spash day has passed. This helps bring more sales and helps you collect more contacts. Building your list is an important part of doing this kind of thing. Make sure people must register with you to get the gifts.

📖 **Monitor your book's ranking on Amazon**

You should check every half hour to watch how it changes. Remember the lower the number, the better. This is where you can find your top-seller or best-seller status.

📖 **Check where your book comes up in its genre or topic area**

Put your keywords or related topics into the Amazon search field. If you come up number one to number ten, you're a top-seller.

📖 **Go to the Best Seller page**

You want to see if your book appears there on your splash day. Remember, this is driven by sales, and the more people you can bring out to buy your book on one day, the better.

📖 Once a best seller, always a Best Seller

Should you achieve the Amazon ranking as a best seller, you can use that on the cover of the book and in all your PR for the life of the book.

📖 📖 📖

Carolyn Howard Johnson, a literary writer, wrote The Frugal Book Promoter to deal with the pitfalls of book promotion and she passes on practical information in her book.

She makes this point clearly, "You can't trace what advertising works. The retail mogul, Bloomingdale said, 'We know advertising works, we just don't know how it works.'

"Some of the things I teach in my UCLA classes, what you can do to increase your chances of success before your book is published, what to do when you have snagged a publisher, and what you can do to keep you book alive an kicking as it starts to get musty on the book stores shelves…the number one freebie thing I like is Amazon, because it gives perks to authors that are absolutely free. I love Listmania…Author's Connect allows to you reach every person who ever purchased your book on Amazon…you can write a "plog" which appears on your book page, and then it goes out to everyone who ever purchased your book. And then, anyone who is interested in getting more plogs can just sign up for it even if they didn't buy your book [on Amazon].

"Some of the very best promotion is that which costs you nothing but time. Nothing is free, there are just some things that cost less than others. But the ones that have always worked the best for me are the ones that are close to free…I spent a $30,000 inheritance for a high powered publicist, even though I was a publicist, I didn't know the book publicist's work. I recognized that I needed something. So, I spent a fortune and she didn't do one thing I couldn't have done myself. If you hire a publicist, you are really hiring their rolodex. You need to hire someone who has all the contacts you'd need…

"Some of the things I do that cost nothing…I write up a review after I've read a book, I trade them for a byline, a thumbnail picture of my book cover or my face and I give them to sites that specialize in reviews. I do the same thing for movies my to local newspapers, and they always run a little tagline saying I'm the author of my books…I always try to tie in my tagline with something in the review.

"One reason I like Amazon so well is that you don't have to be public about it. I suggest that shy writers go take a Toast Master's class to learn how to talk about their books… We are too [filled with our culture] which teaches us from early childhood that there is something wrong with being fond of ourselves, that we are supposed to be humble…I'm not saying there isn't a place for humility, there is. But, if you are passionate enough about your own book that you can talk about it without offending anyone, most people can sense that you are helping someone else. Change your viewpoint in that direction, and you'll find [talking about your books] much easier.

"An author can't trace the results of his efforts. Once in a great while you'll see something that really works…I found that for a non-fiction book it helps to develop followers. After the newsletter, which I developed for authors, and I get new members every week. After the letter comes out, I can see a little spike on Amazon. Once in a while I can see that something worked. But if I did two things in the same week, I can't be sure which one worked or how much...You're not selling a book, you're selling the author. You're selling the brand of the author. Do you know Stephen King? He and his publisher brand 'Stephen King' and they are selling Stephen King. The sales of the books just take care of themselves. His mystique didn't come by accident."

Go to www.carolynhowardjohnson.redenginepress.com/ for more great tips from Carolyn.

And go to http://carolynhoward-johnson.com for more about Carolyn's books.

After all is said and done, selling books boils down to knowing which steps to take, in which order, and for how long. An author will never stop selling his books if he realizes the process is not an overnight one. When an author realizes right away that the success of his book belongs to him, and no one else, then the planning and execution of the plan will pay off.

There are more books that become bestsellers, in the common man's understanding of the word Best Seller, only after years of trial and error in marketing. There are others that find great success outside the bookstore and qualify as best sellers in their own right. It is the author's undying belief in his book that will propel it beyond even his own expectations. But, action must accompany that belief. Anything less is to sell your book short and doom it to the box in the basement and the thought that you wrote a book, but it didn't sell.

PLANNING CHECKLIST — This is very generalized, but it may get you started.

Creation Planning—Fiction

Theme—Started ___/___/___ Completed ___/___/___

Plot Outline—Started ___/___/___ Completed ___/___/___

Character List—Started ___/___/___ Completed ___/___/___

Plot Twists—Started ___/___/___ Completed ___/___/___

Denouement—Started ___/___/___ Completed ___/___/___

Manuscript—Started ___/___/___ Completed ___/___/___

Copyright Forms—Started ___/___/___ Completed ___/___/___

Editor Search—Started ___/___/___ Completed ___/___/___

Creation Planning—Non-Fiction

Theme—Started ___/___/___ Completed ___/___/___

Chapter Outline—Started ___/___/___ Completed ___/___/___

Info List—Started ___/___/___ Completed ___/___/___

Purpose List—Started ___/___/___ Completed ___/___/___

Organization—Started ___/___/___ Completed ___/___/___

Manuscript—Started ___/___/___ Completed ___/___/___

Copyright Forms—Started ___/___/___ Completed ___/___/___

Editor Search—Started ___/___/___ Completed ___/___/___

Marketing Planning—Fiction and Non-Fiction

Publisher Search—Started ___/___/___ Completed ___/___/___

WebDesigner Search—Started ___/___/___ Completed ___/___/___

Manuscript Submission—Started ___/___/___ Completed ___/___/___

Endorsements Search—Started ___/___/___ Completed ___/___/___

Bull's Eye Target—Started ___/___/___ Completed ___/___/___

Media Lists—Started ___/___/___ Completed ___/___/___

Publicist Search—Started ___/___/___ Completed ___/___/___

Booksigning Search—Started ___/___/___ Completed ___/___/___

Library Talks Search—Started ___/___/___ Completed ___/___/___

Radio/TV Interview List—Started ___/___/___ Completed ___/___/___

CHAPTER 7
How will you market your book?

Opportunities are usually disguised as hard work,
so most people don't recognize them.
—Ann Landers, [Esther P. Lederer], 1918-2002

The most serious consideration for all authors, no matter who publishes their book, is the PR budget. Whether you are only marketing to a local demographic and don't intend to pursue broad-based sales of your book, you will still need a budget. This budget is governed by how much you have to spend over a number of months, how much your publisher is planning to spend, and ultimately, how high up the PR food chain you are willing to go.

The Marketing Plan

David Cole, the author of The Complete Guide to Book Marketing, principal of Bay Tree Publishing, and a member of the PMA Board of Directors explains the error most authors make in a nutshell:

"Occasionally, a publisher or a self-published author puts a book in front of me and says, 'I need your help in marketing this book.' I think (but usually refrain from saying out loud), you mean, since you've skipped the marketing process, that you want me to help you sell this book.

"Real marketing begins at the moment a book idea is conceived, and it should affect everything you do. It rests on a clear sense of who the book is for, how it will serve its audience, how and where it will be sold, and how it will compete in the marketplace. It involves—among other things—your choice of title and packaging, as well as the price you charge. Because a conventional marketing plan is usually created downstream chronologically from authorial, editorial, and publishing decisions, people fail to realize that the most important marketing decisions have already been made.

"**You can't repair a marketing mistake by selling harder.** Maybe the idea for your book is so original and timely and the execution is so good that people see it and love it and tell all their friends about it, so that, despite your lack of planning, you have a success. This has happened. Occasionally. But you're more likely to get it right on purpose than by accident. Real marketing begins at the moment a book idea is conceived, and it should affect everything you do."

Dave's list of steps to take is quite long, but really the marketing plan boils down to this concept:

"**The author has to answer two major questions:**

1. How much will you spend on a particular title?

2. And if you target multiple channels, how will you apportion your expenditures?"

It is a given that you will be creating a salable book, qualifying the author by establishing his credibility, establishing a reader profile, choosing an effective title, getting the layout and design to reflect your book in the best possible way. The real work of the marketing plan is the math you will need to work through to get your projections into the realm of reality.

📖 Do the Numbers

Dave points out that "it is essential to do a profit-and-loss statement that accounts for all your expenses and realistically estimates how many books you will sell, and how many you need to sell to break even. With the numbers in hand, you can estimate how much you can reasonably afford to spend on marketing and determine if that sum is enough to let you meet your sales goals."

This takes a lot of guessing and a certain amount of hard reality checking with the author's world of contacts, your own ability to financially support your book, and the publicity projected. Essentially, this is fiction. I prefer to set goals that are achievable, not pie-in-the-sky hype that isn't attainable. And, honestly, authors are not particularly realistic about their books' value in the marketplace or their ability to sell their books. Most authors have it in the back of their minds that their books are going to be the next mega-blockbuster-best-sellers-of-all-time.

Well, I humbly admit, I had these thoughts, too. But, with equal humility, I can now say, I am a skeptic when I hear an author tell me how much his book is going to earn for him and for my company as well. The power of the committed author is not to be ignored. However, there is so much in the process that cannot be controlled, even with a very experienced public relations firm working on your behalf, promotion can come up dry. The desire for success pales fast when the actual attaining of success takes long years of consistent hard work to get the results you hoped you'd achieve in the first six weeks from publication.

📖 The Public Relations Food Chain

Much talk is given to the self-promotion aspects of being an author. Yes, the author's energy, commitment and financial staying power are the key elements in any book's success. And that success may not come for the first book at all until there is a second or third book in the marketplace.

One misconception harbored by new authors is that the larger the publishing house, the more they spend on publicizing your book. Not necessarily so. In fact, in that realm, if the book of a newcomer doesn't set off fireworks in about six weeks, it is left behind, along with the author. Typically, however, the newcomer doesn't even get a chance at the larger firms, simply because the accountants will nix the deal by explaining there is no financial gain in promoting a new author. They stick with their tried and true best selling authors for the most part. Actually, over all, the smaller publishers do a better job working with new authors than the larger houses do.

Bob Gussin, Publisher at Oceanview Publishing, a publisher of adult fiction and non-fiction, started the business after a long career at Johnson and Johnson. I asked Bob to expand on what the small publishers can do that the big firms cannot do.

"The big house's major limitation is getting new material past the financial people. Ninety percent of the time they have to go back to the established authors, even if the work isn't that great. Highly talented authors are not getting published at the big houses. The small publishers have the capability of pushing them. Our greatest opportunity is to find really good talent, pick really good books, and do everything we can within our financial and 'reach' powers to do what we can do for the authors. It is rare that you are going to get a major publisher that will put that kind of effort in. They can put the money in with ads in the New York Times, and if your book takes off like a rocket, they'll continue to do those things. But, even some of the above mid-list authors, their publishers don't set up signings, don't communicate with them. We're not like that, we're a team with our authors."

Oceanview Publishing and Nightengale Press have that teamwork model in common. Many small publishers work hand in hand with their authors to accomplish PR in very creative ways. But, I'd like to provide my view on how PR works.

The PR Pyramid

Let's start at the most accessible level and move upward. Think of publicity as shaped like a pyramid.

The broad base layer can be generated fairly easily and consistently by the author. It is made up of internet press releases, email campaigns, newsletters, direct mail, local news coverage of local booksignings, talks and events, and a publisher provided author website.

The second layer is also relatively easy for the author to use along with help from his publisher. It is made up of paid awards programs, tradeshow placements, author blogs, podcasts, internet radio interviews, online review services, and membership in author organizations.

The third layer is far less accessible, unless the author has a substantial source of funding to expend on paid broadcast radio and television interview placement services, paid print advertising in magazines and newspapers, paid public relations services and publicists, publicized book tours, paying to create an author owned website dedicated to the author and the book, higher level book reviews from major review outlets from publicist placements, major newspaper interviews and coverage of author events, and attendance with a booth at major book tradeshows.

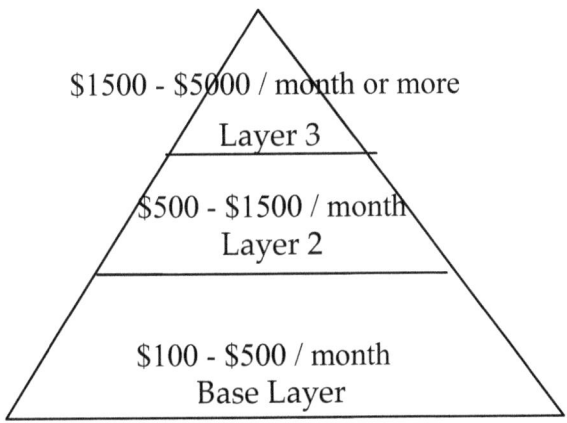

This simple diagram shows in very general terms what these three layers of publicity can cost. Think of each dollar sign as a monthly amount. The Base Layer represents a range of $100 to $500 per month in cost. Layer two represents a range of $500 to $1500 per month in cost. Layer three represents $1500 to $5000 or more per month in cost. In each layer, an author and his publisher may spend more or less per month, but this is a representative range of averages for illustration purposes only. How long the expenses are maintained and how they are allocated varies greatly and are determined by individual circumstances.

Websites can cost quite a bit up front, and then function very reasonably after the initial investment. Most publishers provide a useful website with a bookstore, and often individual sites for authors as part of their services.

📖 Publicists work on monthly retainers, and create campaigns that last for any number of months. Less than three months is too short, but yearly retainers and longterm relationships are possible. Maryglenn McCombs, owner of Maryglenn McCombs Book Publicity, explains the role of the publicist.

"Publicists provide authors with a vital link to consumers. They work to generate coverage in the media that will ideally and hopefully drive customers to stores and outlets where the book is sold. It is a huge job, but a fun one. I work as a liaison between authors and the media, whether it is print media or broadcast media, we work to get reviews, to set up interviews and generate coverage where authors can promote their books to the buying public…It's a numbers game where the odds are not great. When you're competing with thousands of other people who have a book to promote, it is sheer numbers. It is in no way a reflection on your book, but when you think about how much time a book reviewer has to cover books and you look at the huge stack of a thousand books or more per month, it is easy to see why all books are not reviewed. It is hard to get coverage on your own.

"PR people know how to get the book into the right hands…and give reporters a reason to write about the book. We tell them how and why a particular book is relevant to the publication, which allows them to want to write about the book. Self-promotion is very difficult, and it is better to have some one else tout your book for you…There are many ways to think outside the BOOK. Think beyond getting reviews. Can your book make for a great informative short article? Fiction can be very difficult, and so you need to be more creative to find the newsworthy angle and stand alone articles.

"Plan far ahead of the book's publication date—five months or more. The magazines and book trade journals have long lead times. But, if a book is in distribution and it is not selling like you want it to, it is hard to get into the longer lead magazines. Shorter lead print media, newspapers and syndicate radio and some television are a better place to look for that after the pub date coverage. And for serialization, one needs to think in terms of nine months or longer lead time for the magazines which do this... Once your book gets out in the marketplace, but ultimately you are at the consumer's mercy. Whether or not someone chooses to buy your book does not have anything to do with anything you can control."

Email campaigns and newsletters are inexpensive but labor intensive, yet they can be quite effective. Needless to say, radio and television interviews are expensive to generate, unless the book is highly controversial.

Not every book and certainly not every author is going to use the whole pyramid to find an audience for his book. The high end costs are out of reach for most authors and the majority of publishing firms. The budgets of many small publishers are finite and must be carefully allocated to get the most punch for the buck. Using the Publisher's Marketing Association model, the key to high-end publicity is in co-operating as a group to get the conglomerate dollars spent for the most visible exposure.

Authors are frequently unsure of how valuable any particular form of paid services, from print ads to publicists, from email campaigns to paid book tours actually are. It all depends on the book.

📖 One fact is certain: if you don't promote, your book will go unnoticed.

Peter Chamlis is the Advertising Sales Director for ForeWord Magazine, which is a review magazine that targets librarians and booksellers. We talked about cooperative advertising.

"Cooperative advertising strategies work best for small presses and their authors, if they get together and pool their money, they can get much more working together than if they tried to work independently. One of the big advantages to get a whole lot more for a lot less money. Generally, if authors are going to advertise their own titles individually, unless they have a lot of cash, they're going to purchase smaller ads that may not get much notice. If they band together with their publisher, they will get a lot more bang for their buck, and they can compete with the big house ads. The one large disadvantage is that if you have eight, ten, fifteen authors working together, it is a bit like too many cooks can spoil the stew."

The publisher's job is to produce the ad with covers and blurbs, which is an art that most authors don't know how to do. So authors need to trust the publisher in that regard

"And you need consistency. If you allowed twelve people write their own blurbs, well, with the wrong blurb you could have *Gone With the Wind* in the ad and it would say: 'Story about the Civil War,' which is not exactly paying it its due, correct? You want them to look like a collection of equals, though all the subjects are different and may appeal to different kinds of readers, the whole idea of the co-op ad is a series of titles that librarians and booksellers read over and may want to add to their collections...Repetition is very important in advertising, but money talks, and some authors can't afford a year's worth of advertising, so some titles appear only once or twice."

Co-op advertising is tremendously cost effective, we boiled it down to $2.40 a day, which is less than a Starbuck's coffee a day. Can't you put that into your book? It's the idea that co-op ads can be as little as the pocket change we lose between the cushions of our couches.

"Another point is that with a co-op ad compared to a small individual ad, you can do the advertising more inexpensively, but you have a stunning big ad creating the impact," Peter said.

However, authors need to think in terms of a monthly budget of $100 or $200 every month to put into their books.

"A nice consistent plan, like your 'latte' plan is perfect. What makes it work is organization, where people commit to being part of the ad, they get their information to you on time, and they'll pay on time...Before I worked for ForeWord, I was the marketing director for a small press, and I can say there are only two kinds of authors: the kind who will market and the kind who thinks their job is done when the book is published."

Exposure is essential to marketing. Frustrating as can be, it is impossible to track sales from print ads, reviews, magazine and newspaper articles, radio and television appearances, while it is easy to track sales from websites, booksignings and events. But print ads, radio and television appearances, even on local access and small internet stations, do bring exposure to the author and his book. A consumer must see the item three times in three different ways before he connects with the item.

Some authors can even afford television infomercial campaigns and spend millions of dollars on them. We are not talking about that kind of expense in this book as it is really outside the norm.

📖 Bookstores or other venues—which is right for your book?

Deciding where to expend your time, money and energies can take some very hard introspection. Most authors dream of the book tour, with the lines going out the door at big chain bookstores all over the country.

📖 Well, here is the reality

If you are self-published, you or your publisher print your books digitally, you do not have a distributor with a sales force, and you have no budget for publicity, your book will not be on the shelves in bookstores. It may be available upon request, which in itself is a good thing, but the average browsing customer is not going to ask for your book. It's not visible to them, unless you have a very strong booksigning campaign in many bookstores on an on-going basis for months on end.

Bob Gussin of Overview Publishing explains his expereince as a publisher.

"The toughest thing for unknown authors and new publishing companies is the publicity, to become known and to get the book out there broadly. [One] way to sell books is to get the authors out signing. We can see wherever there is a signing we have a spike in sales…You have to stand up, hand the customers a bookmark, hand them the book to show it to them, and get them talking with you. Authors must do all those things at a signing, no sitting back and waiting for customers to come to you…When you get a chance to get out in the public as an author, go to Rotary Clubs, schools, libraries; it is the best way to sell books.

"Almost all of the top authors have been turned down often, J.K. Rowling was rejected forty times…Booksignings are like planting seeds, you have to go out and see people to spread the word about your books. Smaller publishing houses are beneficial for the unknown author, because the bigger houses will drop you like a rock if your book doesn't take off right away, they don't do anything for you. Books do grow over years, so we [smaller publishers] fertilize the fields we're plowing by having our authors participate in panels…we get reviews in smaller papers and magazines, again and again, which has an accumulative effect over time…We hope to make our authors famous, that is our goal. We sign our authors for two books to get the benefit of all the hard work on the first book with your second.

"We have relationships with some of the biggest publishers in New York, we got more time than we thought we would…we were told we're doing what they want to be doing, but because they can't get the unknown author past the money crunchers, they can't take the new authors on."

All authors want to sell more books—many more books. But to create visibility for books, each author needs a variety of approaches to give his book the best possible opportunity to catch on—and to sell. Whether authors have prior or current media access or not, selling books isn't as easy as they thought it might be.

One thing is certain: if you do nothing to promote your book, you will not sell books. Visibility is essential. People need to know who you are to want your book. Gaining consistent and lasting visibility is the real challenge and the real work of being an author. Persistent effort over five years is not unusual to make a book the best seller it will ever be.

While it is potentially easier to sell how-to books and non-fiction, books that provide a clear benefit to the reader directly, fiction has its own appeal, which can still be marketed in a successful way. Just look at all the novels that sell. Just look at all the movies that are made from novels.

MEDIA—the cheapest and best advertising

One obvious alternative is offered by many PR firms, for tens of thousands of dollars per ten-week campaign and with varying guarantees for success. There are thousands to choose from online. Google 'PR firms' and check out their terms. Some promise results or they don't get paid. Some guarantee results, but when you look at the pricing, it is staggering to the typical author.

However, there is much to be learned on these websites, and in talking with these people. An un-ending stream of PR firms approach Nightengale Press several times a week, trying to enlist our business.

Happily, there are effective PR firms that do not charge huge fees, and one in particular is Maryglenn McCombs Book

Publicity. Go to www.maryglenn.com and compare her services with the other firms mentioned above. Her pricing is not listed, mainly because she tailors the costs to the project.

When asked how to determine a publicist is reputable, Maryglenn points out, "All you have to do is ask for references, then email or call them to learn what the publicist did for them, and if they would hire that person again. Ask about the process. How often should I expect to hear from you? When will you pitch to radio or TV? When should I expect to see results? are all questions to ask a prospective publicist. There are so many authors who seek national coverage, most who get on those shows do not start there. Effective book PR takes time and good press begets more press.

To effectively work with a publicist authors need to be available and open to doing things quickly. Also, the author needs to be involved, give input, feedback, suggestions and ideas. It is invaluable."

📖 The first realm of PR is newspaper articles that highlight the author and the book.

This is free advertising. But there has to be a story to tell that makes the newspaper cover the author. Some authors can generate interest but in a limited way. The pursuit of real coverage, in multiple papers requires a relentless routine of press releases, press kits, phone calls and a tirelessly, energetic expenditure of time. Above all, getting a newspaper to write an article requires something unique and unusual for the journalist to talk about. Not just your book. The journalist needs to be able to talk about you, the controversy of your book or the niche your book addresses in a new way.

📖 The second realm of PR is radio interviews that highlight the author and, by the way, the book.

This is also free or nearly free advertising. But, as with the newspaper, there must be a story to tell that makes the radio station want to interview the author. Usually, the interview is about the author, their interesting experience, or life, or the catalyst to the book, and then the book is discussed. There are layers and layers of interview potential too, from Drive Time Talk Radio in the larger cities, to the hundreds of smaller stations that dot the landscape in every state in the country. Of course, the internet offers radio shows too. More on this later in the book.

📖 The third realm of PR is TV interviews, and human interest coverage that highlight the author and, by the way, the book.

This is also free advertising. But, as with the newspaper and radio, there must be a story to tell that makes the TV station want to interview the author. Usually, the interview is about the author, their interesting experience, or life, or the catalyst to the book, and then the book is discussed. As with radio, there are layers and layers of interview potential too, from Morning Talk Shows in larger cities, to the hundreds of smaller local stations that dot the landscape across the nation.

📖 NO ONE IS READY FOR PRIMETIME unless they have played to the smaller markets successfully.

No Broadway play has started out on Broadway. They have to "play in Peoria" first. The great thing about radio is that the interviews can take place by phone. As an example, the technique used by major PR firms is to schedule an author for morning drive time, in all the major market cities, all on the same day. The Author stays at home and talks with the interviewers by phone one after the other all on one day—shotgun media blitz. If you know how to interview, have a great voice and have a clear story to use to sell your book, this can work very well—at least for one day. The follow-up interviews on the local TV stations can take place the same week, but unless the author can travel to the stations, the interview must be by remote hook-up, and that takes money, or a video that is pre-recorded and submitted to play as a spot, again a considerable outlay of money.

📖 Usually the interview show is used to promote a book signing or some event where the author will be appearing soon. So, in the end, the book tour is an essential component to the interview. See the circle? It's like it was for me in the music business in Chicago in the 1990's. If I didn't have a gig, I didn't get a story. If I was working, I got coverage. It's really very simple. The gig gets the interview while the interview feeds getting more gigs.

📖 The most important PR tool is definition of the MARKET

Because the performance factor is at work here, it will be important to start in the smaller markets. This is how the new author gains confidence, hones the patter, refines and perfects what to say. It's a little bit like playing music in your living room for friends, and then in their living rooms for their friends, and finally getting your first gig in a restaurant, and then in a small club, and then in a bigger, better known club, and then on the big stage. No one but a fool would start on the big stage. Go to the smaller radio stations, newspapers and public access cable stations as the first places to begin, spreading the activity further and further a-field from the local scene, to nearby towns, then to the neighboring states, and then back into the larger cities near your locality.

📖 The next most important PR tool is a Great Website

Nightengale Press website provides our authors (as do many publishers) a fully developed website, a comprehensive bookstore, and their own, individual subdomains. Go to www.nightengalepress.com to see what we provide. This is the gateway for sales. It is where clients will come to see you and your publisher. This is a great asset and every publisher of merit provides at least this much for their authors. Self-publishers will need to develop their own sites. Also, go to serveral publisher websites to see how they present theirs and take components that work for your book and build them into your website. See the information at the end of this chapter and in Chapter 12 for details about how to do this and where to find useful providers.

📖 EVERYTHING HINGES ON the Author Event component

"How-to and Non-fiction" authors will need to develop a speaking/demonstration tour in the local businesses and stores that pertain to their books.

"Children's" authors will need to develop a reading tour in local libraries, elementary schools and bookstore children sections.

All authors, and expecially "Fiction" authors will need to develop book signings in book stores, but can also give talks in libraries, schools and at author's groups.

📖 "Meet the Author" and local book club affiliations are growing fast. For Children's book writers, Children'slit.com is a place to list yourself for events and groups. Go to www.childrenslit.com/f_mai.htm. Developing a book club following would also be a good idea. There are many small groups of people who get together to read books, finding one (or more) to read your book would be a great idea. Look into the Reader's Circle at www.readerscircle.org/authors.html to begin, or just type Local Book clubs into the Google search engine for lots of options.

📖 The following EXAMPLES illustrate how authors in different genre can develop their events.

📖 HEATH & FITNESS AUTHORS
HEATH & FITNESS LINKS:

This link provides a complete nationwide state-by-state listing of ALL the clubs.
www.healthclubdirectory.com/health_clubs/United_States/

📖 CHILDREN'S AUTHORS
TEACHER STORES:

These links provide a copious listing of teacher stores throughout the United States. These are all potential retail outlets for children's books.
www.elp-web.com/pages/dealers.htm#IL
www.teacherstores.com/

SCHOOL DISTRICTS:

These links provide extensive information and listings about school districts in the USA. Useful for getting contact information for arranging school readings of your books. This is a great way to interest kids, teachers and parents. Schools are often looking for willing authors to read their books to elementary children. You may not be paid for the presentation, but you will sell books.

www.education-world.com/regional/north_america/k12_schools/usa/

www.k2nesoft.com/education.html

ALL AUTHORS LIBRARIES:

Where you can give talks and readings for free, but again you'll be developing your audience. It's a great way to network in your community, and those around you. The people you meet can lead you to other venues as well. Remember, it is all about visibility. Also, library presentations validate you as an author. If the librarians like you, it's a great item to put on your resume, and helps you gain signing entrance to local bookstores.

Libraries in all countries:

www.sunsite3.berkeley.edu/Libweb/

BOOK STORES:

In the USA: Borders, Barnes & Noble, Waldenbooks, and GOOGLE the independent booksellers

In CANADA:

www.cbabook.org/find/default.asp

Scroll down on this page to find the names and addresses of booksellers in Canada—very useful.

IN AUSTRALIA:
www.anulib.anu.edu.au/elibrary/books.html
Full listing of book stores in Australia. All of these could potentially carry your books, and publishers are usually willing to communicate with these stores to place your books.

📖 BOOK CLUBS
Your local libraries are also great resources for finding the book clubs in your immediate area. Your publisher should be willing to offer your titles at a discount, and it is potentially one of the best ways for you to get known in your locale.

In the US: GOOGLE the term Book Clubs—the listings are incredible.
In Australia:
www.scholastic.com.au/schools/bookclub/
In Canada:
www.canadianbookclubs.com/Canada.html

📖 TARGETED CO-OPERATIVE ADVERTISING—The cheapest and best high end advertising

Advertising dollars are considerably easier to spend than almost any other money in book promotion. The key is to get some return on those dollars. If booksellers and librarians see your books frequently in the important trade journals and in mailings (email or direct mail) meant specifically for them, they will respond. If they never see your titles in these venues, then they will not find you as easily.

Publishers Marketing Association Programs: PMA marketing programs offer ooperative mailings, staffed exhibits, and catalog mailings allow you to benefit from PMA's experience, reputation and positive image while sharing costs with other publishers. These programs have been proven and refined over the years. They'll help your sales grow efficiently and cost effectively. Ask your publisher about cooperative advertising opportunities offered to all the authors under that imprint. Nightengale Press routinely seeks advertising agreements to benefit all our authors. Through PMA you can also present your titles at national, regional and international book fairs through staffed exhibits. PMA arranges for booth space at these major book trade shows and member publishers may either opt to purchase multiple, full or shared booth space within the PMA complex or show their titles within the PMA cooperative booths.

📖 TRADESHOWS

Peter Chamlis of Foreword Magazine explains their tradeshow services. They represent titles at BookExpoAmerica, Frankfurt, London, Bologna, and Beijing.

"Frankfurt Book Fair (in October) is filled with agents and sub-agents who are looking for books to acquire for foreign rights and translation rights. They know exactly what they're looking for, they aren't looking for your welcome, you let them browse and if they ask you a few questions, it is not a real wordy exchange that happens. The size of the show is incredible. Anyone walking into the English Language Hall looking to do business has a grasp of English. They want to quietly thumb through the titles. For some reason those interested in the genre of Mind/Body/Spirit, I seem to attract people interested in these titles. They tell you what they're interested in, but your customers are more informed and know what they want. The show was packed, and the traffic came in waves, but it is like there are large groups of people working their way through the hall. There are ten different halls, each housing titles grouped by language.

"All tradeshows provide the chance for titles to be seen, especially for smaller presses. Larger houses set up with many titles, but they are doing the same kind of thing. Agents come to find out what is new and what may translate in other languages. The first step is you have to be seen. It is not a sure thing, not by a long shot. Perhaps fifteen or twenty percent of titles will generate interest, but if your title is not there, it will not generate any interest. There are never guarantees in advertising, tradeshows, the lottery, or anything else. You must be on the radar to be seen."

REVIEWS

How, where Where and Why you want your book reviewed, if you believe your book will qualify, in a trade journal.

The trade journals are the big guys in the review world, and they have rather stringent guidelines for getting reviews. I recommend when you are reading a book that your read these review blurbs in your favorite author's book, and you'll see whether or not your author is up to getting that top billing.

"*Great Novel!*" or "*Interesting!*" or "*Spell-binding!*" These one word captions come from a review and it tells you where it came from. Notice, too, that it is one word or a short phrase from the review. This is how you quote only the best part of the review on your book.

If you get a good review in one of the trade journals such as: The Library Journal, The School Library Journal, Kirkus

Reviews, or Publisher's Weekly, this will almost instantly translate into sales. Getting a good review in other good publishing periodicals like ForeWord Magazine or Independent Publisher can also help with your sales because these are all recognized magazines that go out to the trade. Unfortunately, these publications get thousands of books a week and can only review a few dozen at most. So how does a small publisher, a medium sized publisher or a self-publisher make a book stand out and garner that review attention? There are three main tips, and if you're an author, you need to think about as you are writing and producing your book.

Tip One: Create a good book with quality writing, quality material, depth of coverage are very important in fiction. For non-fiction, present compelling new information or solve a problem the reader has come to you to get the answer for.

Tip Two: Know each publication. Go to the websites of each publication and read the actual magazines, perhaps at the library, because it is not a good idea to send your book for review if you don't know what the purpose of the magazine you are submitting to actually is.

Tip Three: Follow the submission guidelines. These are available on the webistes. If you miss the requirements they ask of you, then they will just toss your book away.

Other important tips:

Publish your book in the off season, such as in August, December, January or February.

📖 **Follow submission guideline instructions exactly.**
📖 **Submit one or two copies of your Galley** (the pre-publication proof which still probably has typos) three to four months ahead of publication. There will still be mistakes in the book but it is in the layout and design of your book, but reviewers don't care about that.
📖 **This galley can be printed** from your computer, but it must be bound at a copy center.
📖 **Trade journals want their reviews** to appear BEFORE the book is available, and they NEVER review a book after publication. There are other ways to get post- publication reviews.
📖 **A Self-published book must have a print run** of at least two thousand books, be represented by a reputable distributor (Ingram, Baker & Taylor, BookWorld are three). You will not get your books into bookstores without a distributor.
📖 **You get only one shot at reviews.** Once it is accepted or rejected, that is it. You can't submit it again.
📖 **Most will review both** paperback and hardcover books in all subject areas.
📖 **Get endorsements** from people in the genre or subject area to qualify your book.
📖 **You must have significant publicity** and advertising plans with exposure to the marketplace.
📖 **followup your submission** according to the publication's guidelines, typically they allow one email, one faxed inquiry, or no followup at all. None of them accept phone calls.
📖 **Getting reviews is all in the details.** Send it to the publication(s) that review(s) your kind of book, craft a good cover letter, make sure your book is well made, and some good luck.

HERE'S WHAT A BOOK GOES THROUGH TO GET A REVIEW AT FOREWORD MAGAZINE:

Nightengale Press submits select titles for review to ForeWord Magazine, with the purpose of gaining reviews for some of our forthcoming titles. This is a free service. Not all authors' books will be reviewed, and not all books will be represented, but the goal is to get the reviews rolling and gain more and more success for our authors in this realm. These representations must be made while books are still forthcoming, and we will certainly choose the "hottest" of our titles for this purpose.

Alex Moore, Executive Director at Foreword Magazine explained the review process of how mainstream reviews are decided upon. He was a book packager for eight years, so he has been scrutinizing books for many years.

"Foreword reviews books from independent publishers and university presses, and the audience is librarians and booksellers, with 75% of the audience being librarians. We prepare reviews that we think have value and distinction and have imaginative power. Book reviews should be essays that people enjoy reading even if they never even buy the books. When they are very good reviews, books may sell. We only review worthy books. There is no use writing a negative review and taking up space where a positive review could go.

"We get about 1600 books every two months and we review about 4% because of print space. Reviews are divided in twenty categories, such as Arts, Business and Careers etc...as in the normal bookstores. We have about a hundred reviewers, quite a few are college professors, some are freelancers who like to write reviews in specialties, others are journalists with good credentials which helps with the credibility of the reviews.

"We have very detailed guidelines, and we compare reviews. I want a description so the readers can determine that the book is something they'd really like to purchase. When I get the reviews, I coach the reviewer, then it comes back to me again, then it goes to my assistant, and then it goes to the real editor, our chopper, who really edits the review. She critiques it and sends it back to me for approval. There needs to be a good value to the review with a bit of creativity, some finesse and a flourish to make the reviews of value. It is invigorating, I learn a lot but it does take some time.

"Non-fiction books have to be considered for subject matter, presentation, the author's credentials, whether it is repetitive—has been written before, if it has a good title and subtitle that catches my attention.

"Fiction titles are more fun, like tasting wine. Oscar Wilde said one time, 'You don't have to drink the whole cask to tell if the wine is good. Maybe in a half an hour you can tell if a book is good.' Naturally, I can't read the whole book. I have to sample it, so I have to be able to tell in a minute or so whether the book really qualifies. Sometimes I get drawn in, and it typically meets the standards I'm looking for.

"On the other hand, if the first page has a lot of 'I's or 'but's, words that are echoing and that are repetitive, if they add up to something that is not so good, the book doesn't get reviewed. If the pace is slow, if there is too much explanation, too many adjectives, and clichés are the worst enemy. The cumulative effect is what matters. Precise word choice is very important. Imagination and a good turn of phrase is important. If the sentences are rhythmically unpleasant, I know the author hasn't worked on it. I want a little panache. I add up all these nuances and if they are positive, then the book will be reviewed, allowing for space and the editorial calendar's requirements."

I asked Alex about the differences between literary fiction and popular fiction.

"Literary fiction is driven by the examination of character, but the writers use of language is also clearly more diligently worked upon for the details I listed before. Popular fiction is more driven by plot, and it is entertaining for that reason.

"You are what you read, and you will write what you read, at least there is going to be a difference in the product if you are more involved as a reader of popular fiction than a writer who reads primarily literature."

Then I asked Alex what happens when a book does get selected for review.

"If a book is selected, I put it aside and send it to the reviewer I think would do a good job with that book. When it comes back in, I screen it, my assistant prepares it and Karen McCarthy edits it. A good review goes to the publisher before we publish it to make sure the ISBN and price are accurate. Foreword is a pre-publication review journal. We get the galleys early and there are sometimes changes in the book. The publisher can use blurbs from the review on press releases, on second printings, in any way they choose.

There are 175,000 to 200,000 books produced each year, and there are only ten pre-publication review magazines, but in spite of the fact that the percentages are small, if you get the review, it can be used for years and even on the second title."

All reviews can be presented in your press kit, and as you develop a number of articles about your book, reviews of your book and exposure grows for your book, your press kit will help you get more radio and television coverage of your book, as long as you have a substantial publicity campaign to support it.

The timeline for building your book's credibility begins the moment you begin to write it. The marketing plan, your media plan, your reviews, your awareness that all these things begin as you are writing your book will better serve its success. You do not have to be thinking "major markets" to create a successful title that has good sales strength. But, you do have to plan for the process you are going to take your book through to get that sales strength. If this chapter has provided you anything, I hope it has provided you the information and guidelines you need to follow to get the most from your book.

BEYOND THE TRADE

There are book-specific review services like BookPage, Bloomsbury Review, New York Review of Book, and Pages. Remember the major newspapers' book review sections: the New York Times Book Review, Los Angeles Times Book Review, the Washington Post Book Review, the Chicago Tribune Book Review and of course, the regional and local papers as well.

There are also numerous online review services that accept galleys and take books after publication as well, which and whose guidelines are less stringent. These are typically fee based and charge from $75 to $350 per review. You can Google these services by putting Online Reviewers into the search bar.

So many first-time authors think they will get book reviews once their book is published. They blindly buy hundreds of books to send out for review only to discover they should have done this step before the release of the book. I cannot stress this enough. Publicity starts while you are writing the book!

Okay, but what do you do if you skipped this step and

have a bunch of books to use to get reviews? Happily, there are online review services that will review post publication books. The big time review services like Publisher's Weekly, Kirkus Reviews, ForeWord Magazine, and so on will not review books that are past their pub-dates. Typically, these services will review primarily mainstream books, submitted by established publicity services. So, what is the self-published, POD printed, small press to do?

Of course, you can Google: book review services and find more than you'll know what to do with. The following are a representative selection which Nightengale Press has used, or which come highly recommended as among the best. When it comes to paying for a review, rest assured, everyone is concerned that the result will be a glowing review, even if the book isn't so good. Not so. But to the contrary, one that is a not-so-good review in the eyes of the author, may seem like an interesting review to a potential reader. Remember the controversy that sprung up around the *DaVinci Code* by Dan Brown. Many reviews panned the writing, but loved the intrigue. The religious community was up in arms over the premise of the book. Fiction with political/cultural teeth sells, even if it isn't literature. A bad review may actually be a good review. Odd, but true.

Even so, these services also are well employed before your book is published to garner more mainstream media coverage. If your book is submitted to a for-fee review service first, this does not necessarily mean it will not qualify for a traditional outlet review. Carefully selected quotes from these reviews can be used as a "what they are saying about" your book sheet that in turn should accompany your book to the more traditional reviewers at newspapers, magazines, and industry publications. They may tip the balance in your book's favor.

FOR FEE REVIEW SERVICES

www.kirkusdiscoveries.com
For-fee Review Service, $350 per title

For the first time in seventy-three years, Kirkus is offering a new review service, giving a whole new class of writers the opportunity to get attention for their books and giving rights and acquisitions agents the chance to watch out for books that might interest them. Any book is fair game, whether conventionally published, self-published, e-published, published via Print-On-Demand, or not previously published at all.

Kirkus Discoveries is a paid review service that allows authors and publishers of overlooked titles to receive authoritative, careful assessment of their books. Here's how it works:

A review is commissioned ($350 per title) from the Discoveries team, who assigns the book to one person within the Kirkus pool of professional reviewers, who in turn provides an honest, caveat-emptor evaluation, under the same impartial rubric as Kirkus Reviews.

The power of the name Kirkus stands strong with this service. Yes, you pay for the review, and what you get is an honest appraisal, not a guaranteed glowing review. Impartiality is most important in the review process, and Kirkus has a reputation to uphold. These reviews cost more, but they are professionally written by seasoned reviewers. Well worth the price.

www.forewordmagazine.com/clarion/
for-fee service, $305 per title

If you are an author or publisher experiencing trouble getting your titles reviewed through traditional outlets, consider Clarion, a fee for review service now offered through ForeWord. For $305, a professional review of your title, with the same quality and word length offered in the magazine, and very often by the same reviewers (or those used by PW, Library Journal, Kirkus and Booklist) is now available.

Paying $305 for a professional 400+ word critique is the best marketing value available in this industry. Use the review in your press kit, blurb your cover, highlight in your marketing campaigns. With your permission, the review will be archived with the top three title information databases used by booksellers and librarians who make purchasing decisions: Bowker's Books-In-Print online, Baker & Taylor's Titlesource 3, and Ingram's iPage, in addition to www.forewordmagazine.com.

www.pma-online.com
for-fee, $210 per title, Authors of Member Publishers Only

PMA designs newsletter-type catalog sheets which feature a front cover picture of your book, along with a 100-word description. Also included are ISBN, price, a maximum of three distributors/wholesalers, and publishing company's name and address (which is not included as part of the 100-word description). All descriptive paragraphs will be edited to meet the 100-word requirement.

Books for Review:
Currently mailed every-other-month (January, March, May, July, September, November) to approximately 3,500 metro and weekly newspaper book reviewers across the U.S. Mailing list is purchased from Standard Rate and Data Service. Bounce-back cards are included in this mailing for reviewer to request specific title(s). Names, addresses and phone numbers of requesting reviewer is forwarded to each participating publisher. Program mails 3rd class and each participant receives a copy first class.

What to Expect from Cooperative Catalog Mailings: Best case: Many review requests and orders from libraries and bookstores. Average case: A modest amount of review requests and orders from libraries and bookstores over the next six months. Worst case: Exposure to the market.

If the 100-word description does its job, requests come through, and in a couple of months, the PMA member receives a review that may or may not go into the publication that wrote it. This process is less direct and more anonymous than the other services are, and so, because it is more hit-or-miss, some books are not reviewed even though the fee is paid.

It is important to note that a volunteer pool of avid readers, who are not paid to write for-fee reviews, is going to produce reviews that may well hit the mark in a positive way, or they may not. Most are excellent and well written. If the author is unhappy with a review, some services will offer the book to another reviewer to provide a second reading, free of charge.

www.ReaderViews.com
For-fee Review Service, sliding scale of costs

Reader Views, a volunteer based site, is here to help you. Our book reviews are written by avid readers who love to read good books. They come from all walks of life with a variety of life experiences and interests. Our readers are volunteers hand picked to give you the best review possible. They give their own honest and fair personal opinion.

FREE ONLINE REVIEW SERVICES

Free book reviews written by everyday people can tell an author, and the media, what the readers-at-large are going to think about a particular book. These services provide well written reviews that thoughtfully critique the book in a constructive way. Even if the review is over all very positive, these reviewers do add constructive criticism where appropriate.

www.midwestbookreviews.com
Free Review Service

"Established in 1976, the Midwest Book Review publishes several monthly publications for community and academic library systems in California, Wisconsin, and the upper Midwest:

"The Bookwatch, California Bookwatch, Children's Bookwatch, Internet Bookwatch, Library Bookwatch , MBR Bookwatch, Reviewer's Bookwatch, Small Press Bookwatch, Wisconsin Bookwatch. We post all our reviews on the Internet with a number of thematically appropriate areas of the Internet such as www.alt.books.reviews and Pub-Forum. Our reviews are also available through Internet bookstores such as Amazon.com."

www.frontStreetReviews.com
Free Review Service

"Front Street Reviews is the road to follow for anyone who loves books. Every day there are new books on the market, new authors to try, new genres to explore (I mean where was "chick lit" or "paranormal romance" five years ago?) In our busy lives it is increasingly hard to find the time we need to test read it all. Front Street Reviews is here to give you sign posts through the process. By previewing and providing information on the books and their authors we make sure you can spend your time reading the books you will really enjoy.

"At the same time, we realize that each book is a part of its author heart and soul. It is our goal to match books with the readers that will best appreciate them. Our honest, thorough reviews do just that."

AMAZON.COM Reviews.

Though often these reviews are submitted by readers known to the authors, and therefore are not considered serious reviews, some of the online review services routinely submit their reviews to the book's listing on Amazon as a means to better qualify the title. Midwest Book Reviews, Readerviews.com and FrontStreetReviews.com all do this. If you have a major trade review, you or your publisher can post it on your Amazon listing, your Barnes & Noble listing and all the other online stores as well.

Now, having said all this, there is nothing that feels better to an author than the validation that comes from a well-written, thoughtful, usable review. It can appear on the author's website, it can be excerpted for the "Praise Sheet" part of a press kit, included in press releases, put on posters and bookmarks handed out at book signings, added to the back cover of the book, and used for any other purpose you can think up. Maybe reviews don't sell books, but they do draw attention.

AWARDS

This is another way to bring validation and credibility to your book and to yourself as an author. If you Google book awards and the year you'll find about **70,600,000** options for book awards each year. For the ultimate in information about major awards in many categories including the Pulitzer Prize go to www.bookspot.com and www.bookreporter.com. Both these sites reflect the mainstream publishing world, and while your book might not fit the guidelines, it is educational to see what these organizations are looking for.

But, for those in the independent publishing community and self-publishers, there are five prestigious awards that are accessible to your books. They all have moderate entrance fees, guidelines and requirements, but they are meant for writers like you. Just because you enter doesn't mean you'll win, or even be a finalist. But, the chance taken is well worth any fee. Just as being nominated for an Oscar brings honor to those in the film community, being a finalist for these awards is nearly as useful as being in the winner's circle. And, while you have one shot per year, it is worth the effort to enter.

There are award programs that highlight the year's best titles, which are typically timed to call for entries late in the eligible copyright year so they can be announced at BookExpoAmerica in the late spring.

Other award programs, typically genre related, provide validation anytime of the year and act like the Good House Keeping Seal of Approval for titles wearing the medallions that shine like a beacon in the night from the front cover of the book. Any award is a good thing, and while some are more recognizable than others, it is always good to have an award telling the potential buyer the book has been judged worthy of recognition.

You can simply Google your genre or topic with the word "awards" and you'll have more than you know what to do with. Most awards require payment of an entrance fee, and of course, you must send in books and press releases, any articles that feature your title and the like.

THE BOOK OF THE YEAR AWARDS sponsored by ForeWord Magazine. www.forewordmagazine.com

"Any independently published titles in any format with a copyright date of 2006 are eligible to enter. New editions of previously published books are eligible.

"The Book of the Year Awards program was designed specifically for booksellers and librarians to share in the process of discovering distinctive books across a number of genres with judgments based on their own authority in each category and on patron/customer interests. These carefully chosen titles affirm our notion that the best ideas in written form are coming from the independent press community, and that with some distinction, will find a broader audience among the reading public."

📖 **THE BENJAMIN FRANKLIN AWARDS** sponsored by Publisher's Marketing Association. www.pma-online.org

"The awards recognize excellence in both editorial and design. The specific genre categories are judged by three industry professionals, coming from the library, bookstore, reviewer, designer, publicity and editorial markets. The comments from these judges are returned to all participants at the completion of the competition. This awards program is the only one that allows you to receive direct comments from the people who will make the buying and/or review decisions on your product."

📖 **THE IPPY AWARDS** sponsored by the Independent Publisher Online and Jenkins Group, Inc. www.independentpublisher.com

"For eleven years the Independent Publisher Book Awards have been conducted annually to honor the year's best independently published titles. The "IPPY" Awards reward those who exhibit the courage, innovation, and creativity to bring about change in the world of publishing. Independent spirit and expertise comes from publishers of all sizes and budgets, and books are judged with that in mind. All independent, university, small press, and self-publishers who produce books intended for the North American market are eligible to enter titles copyrighted or released in 2006. Independent authors using print-on-demand publishing services are welcome to enter their books themselves."

📖 **THE PARENT TO PARENT ADDING WISDOM AWARD**™
www.addingwisdomaward.com

"Established in 1998, by syndicated family/health columnist and author, Jodie Lynn, this award honors products of outstanding quality that support family values and includes websites. The Adding Wisdom Award™ committees include experts from across the United States who are involved with children on a daily basis and look for products that entertain and teach, inspiring imagination and creativity. Additionally, they are interested in how products help children, as well as, everyday families, grow ethically, socially, intellectually, emotionally and physically. Products are given to Family Testers for testing and evaluation before final decisions are reached. New categories have recently been added: Cook Books, Business Books, Getting Organized and Household Tools. Parent to Parent Adding Wisdom Award™ is the only award program to ever be honored by Disney.com."

All of this can be particularly overwhelming when you approach the idea of sending your book out for scrutiny by strangers, for judgment by experts, or dissemination for the world. But, taking risks are a large part of creating success for any book, and authors are the ones who put their creative souls on the line each and every time they submit a press release, try to get a review or enter their work in a contest to get an award. Still, taking the risk is the price authors must pay for their books, otherwise, they might as well just leave them unwritten.

📖 📖 📖

As you write your book, the first Publicity Timeline should give you a basic plan to follow as your book evolves.

📖 📖 📖

If your book is already written, the second Publicity Timeline will help you design a clear plan to follow to increase your marketing reach.

📖 📖 📖

📖 FIRST PUBLICITY TIMELINE 📖

Book Concept_____
Set Pub Date ____/____/____
Reader Portrait_____
_____

Marketing Budget
$_____.00 per month for Publicist for _____months. Rehire for ____months.

Publicity firms you are considering:
1)_____
2)_____
3)_____

What you want the firm to accomplish:

Press Fact Sheet
      Author Bio
        Accomplishments
        Awards
Praise Sheet
      Reviews
      Endorsements

Press Releases on a six month timeline

Web-based media services:
1)_____
2)_____
3)_____

📖 **PRINT MEDIA CAMPAIGN**
📖 **Newspapers**
Local:
1)_____
2)_____
3)_____
Regional:
1)_____
2)_____
3)_____
National:
1)_____
2)_____
3)_____
3)_____
4)_____
5)_____
6)_____

📖 **NOTES:**

📖 Magazines

Local:
1)_____
2)_____
3)_____

Regional:
1)_____
2)_____
3)_____

National:
1)_____
2)_____
3)_____
3)_____
4)_____
5)_____
6)_____

📖 NOTES:

📖 EVENTS AND INTERVIEWS

$_____.00 per month for Radio/TV interviews/ADS and Appearance Fees
Station:_____
Station:_____
Station:_____
Station:_____
Station:_____

📖 BOOKSTORE BOOKSIGNINGS
$_____.00 per month for Travel to Booksignings

Store:_____
INCOME from Signing:
Store:_____
INCOME from Signing:
Store:_____
INCOME from Signing:
Store:_____
INCOME from Signing:
Store:_____
INCOME from Signing:

📖 SPEAKING / Libraries, Organizations, Schools
$_____.00 per month for books for Back of the Room Sales

Library:_____
INCOME from Signing:
Library:_____
INCOME from Signing:

CALLING ALL AUTHORS—Valerie Connelly

Organization:_____
INCOME from Signing:
Organization:_____
INCOME from Signing:

School:_____
INCOME from Signing:
School:_____
INCOME from Signing:

📖 NOTES:

📖 REVIEWS AND AWARDS

Submit Galleys to Mainstream Review Journals at least 5 months before pub date if your book is available directly to the trade through a distributor and is printed offset.

📖 Publisher's Weekly
Registered
Submitted
Tracked

📖 Kirkus Reviews
Registered
Submitted
Tracked

📖 Library Journal
Registered
Submitted
Tracked

📖 School Library Journal
Registered
Submitted
Tracked

📖 Foreword Magazine
Registered
Submitted
Tracked

📖 Submit Galleys to Online For a Fee Review Websites at least 3 months before pub date if your book is not available directly through a distributor and is printed digitally. (This does not include Ingram and Baker & Taylor availability)

📖 www.kirkusdiscoveries.com
Registered
Submitted
Tracked

📖 www.forwordmagazine.com/clarion
Registered
Submitted
Tracked

📖 www.readerviews.com
Registered
Submitted
Tracked

📖 www.frontStreetReviews.com
Registered
Submitted
Tracked

📖 www.pma-online.com
Registered
Submitted
Tracked

Research Awards in your genre or topic aread for more opportunities. Work with your publisher to submit your books to these awards.

BOOK OF THE YEAR AWARDS www.forewordmagazine.com

THE BENJAMIN FRANKLIN AWARDS www.pma-online.org

THE IPPY AWARDS www.independentpublisher.com

THE PARENT TO PARENT ADDING WISDON AWARD www.addingwisdomaward.com

📖 SECOND PUBLICITY TIMELINE 📖

Book Concept_____
Set Pub Date ____/____/____
Reader Portrait_____
_____

📖 Marketing Budget
$_____.00 per month for Publicity for _____months. Renew for ____months.

What you PLAN to accomplish:

Develop Your Press Fact Sheet
    Author Bio
    Accomplishments
    Awards
Develop Your Praise Sheet
    Reviews
    Endorsements

📖 Write Press Releases on a six month timeline
Press Release 1:_____
_____
Press Release 2:_____
_____
Press Release 3:_____
_____
Press Release 4:_____
_____
Press Release 5:_____
_____

📖 **WEB-BASED MEDIA OUTLETS: You may find others as well**

📖 **PRACTICE** www.prfree.com—no fee

Release Title:_____
Registered
Submitted
Tracked

Release Title:_____
Registered
Submitted
Tracked

Release Title:_____
Registered
Submitted
Tracked

📖 **PUBLICIZE** www.prweb.com—$40 minimum fee/$80 to get higher placement

Release Title:_____
Registered
Submitted
Tracked

Release Title:_____
Registered
Submitted
Tracked

Release Title:_____
Registered
Submitted
Tracked

Release Title:_____
Registered
Submitted
Tracked

Release Title:_____
Registered
Submitted
Tracked

Release Title:_____
Registered
Submitted
Tracked

Release Title:_____
Registered
Submitted
Tracked

Release Title:_____
Registered
Submitted
Tracked

EZINES AND ARTICLES

www.ezinearticles.com
Registered and set up site ____/____/____

Article Title:_____
Registered
Submitted
Tracked

Article Title:_____
Registered
Submitted
Tracked

Article Title:_____
Registered
Submitted
Tracked

Article Title:_____
Registered
Submitted
Tracked

Article Title:_____
Registered
Submitted
Tracked

📖 www.authorsden.com
Registered and set up site ____/____/____

Article Title:_____
Registered
Submitted
Tracked

Article Title:_____
Registered
Submitted
Tracked

Article Title:_____
Registered
Submitted
Tracked

Article Title:_____
Registered
Submitted
Tracked

Article Title:_____
Registered
Submitted
Tracked

📖 PRINT MEDIA CAMPAIGN
Newspapers
Local:
1)_____
2)_____
3)_____
Regional:
1)_____
2)_____
3)_____
National:
1)_____
2)_____
3)_____
3)_____
4)_____
5)_____
6)_____

📖 NOTES:

📖 Magazines
Local:
1)_____
2)_____
3)_____
Regional:
1)_____
2)_____
3)_____
National:
1)_____
2)_____
3)_____
3)_____
4)_____
5)_____
6)_____

📖 NOTES:

📖 EVENTS AND INTERVIEWS

$_____.00 per month for Radio/TV interviews/ADS and Appearance Fees
Station:_____
Station:_____
Station:_____
Station:_____
Station:_____

📖 BOOKSTORE BOOKSIGNINGS
$_____.00 per month for Travel to Booksignings

Store:_____
INCOME from Signing:
Store:_____
INCOME from Signing:
Store:_____
INCOME from Signing:
Store:_____
INCOME from Signing:
Store:_____
INCOME from Signing:

📖 SPEAKING / Libraries, Organizations, Schools
$_____.00 per month for books for Back of the Room Sales

Library:_____
INCOME from Signing:
Library:_____
INCOME from Signing:

Organization:_____
INCOME from Signing:
Organization:_____
INCOME from Signing:
School:_____
INCOME from Signing:
School:_____
INCOME from Signing:

📖 NOTES:

📖 REVIEWS AND AWARDS

Submit Galleys to Mainstreant Review Journals at least 5 months before pub date if your book is available directly to the trade through a distributor and is printed offset.

📖 Publisher's Weekly
Registered
Submitted
Tracked

📖 Kirkus Reviews
Registered
Submitted
Tracked

📖 Library Journal
Registered
Submitted
Tracked

📖 School Library Journal
Registered
Submitted
Tracked

📖 Foreword Magazine
Registered
Submitted
Tracked

📖 Submit Galleys to Online For a Fee Review Websites at least 3 months before pub date if your book is not available directly through a distributor and is printed digitally. (This does not include Ingram and Baker & Taylor availability)

📖 www.kirkusdiscoveries.com
Registered
Submitted
Tracked

📖 www.forwordmagazine.com/clarion
Registered
Submitted
Tracked

📖 www.readerviews.com
Registered
Submitted
Tracked

📖 www.frontStreetReviews.com
Registered
Submitted
Tracked

📖 www.pma-online.com
Registered
Submitted
Tracked

📖 Research Awards in your genre or topic aread for more opportunities. Work with your publisher to submit your books to these awards.

BOOK OF THE YEAR AWARDS www.forewordmagazine.com

THE BENJAMIN FRANKLIN AWARDS www.pma-online.org

THE IPPY AWARDS www.independentpublisher.com

THE PARENT TO PARENT ADDING WISDOM AWARD www.addingwisdomaward.com

WHETHER YOU ARE USING THE FIRST PUBLICITY TIMELINE OR THE SECOND PUBLICITY TIMELINE YOU WILL NEED A WEBSITE AND A BLOG

📖 **YOUR WEBSITE:** Your publisher may supply one, but you can have more than one, even a separate website for each book you write and for you as an author. Your website(s) are where you will draw more attention to you and your book and process direct sales. This takes time and energy.

📖 Choose WEB HOST and register your unique domain name: GoDaddy.com

📖 Decide how you will develop your site:Do It yourself:

1) Yahoo Sitebuilder: Go to Yahoo.com and click on Webhosting
2) Macromedia provides excellent website software, but you need serious computer skills for this profession application.
If you are not real computer savvy, get someone to develop your website for you.
Cost: $200 - $5000. This depends on many factors, including whether the site is developed in .HTML or FLASH, has video capacity, is multi layered, or just a few pages, is high maintenance or one time set up.

📖 **Design considerations:** Color scheme, photos, videos, content, pdf downloads, music, purpose, bookstore or link to your publisher's bookstore.
Go To www.nightengalepress.com Author's Directory to see our author's websites.
Go To www.dyingtobeyoung.net, www.headlineit.net, and www.surrogacywastheway.com, to see some of our author's stand-alone websites.

📖 **YOUR BLOG:** Where you will draw more attention to you and your book. These are much easier to develop and use than websites, but they do not replace your website. Blogs are a great addition to your internet presence. You can do this for yourself at no cost.

Set up with blog software available online with one of these providers. They are excellent.
www.blogger.com
www.wordpress.com
Follow the setup instructions, and learn how to do this. It takes a little time to get used to the process, but then it is easy to use regularly.

📖 **NOTES:**

CHAPTER 8
Printing—since the Gutenburg Bible

The oldest books are still only just out to those who have not read them.
—Samuel Butler, 1835-1902

For the typical writer, how his book is printed may be immaterial; he just wants to see it in print. Yet, for the publisher, the marketplace and the consumer, how a book is printed makes all the difference in the world. The evolution of printing, since the first practical press was invented in Germany by the goldsmith and printer Johannes Gutenburg in ca. 1447, has produced sequentially greater productivity and wider readership with increasingly faster creation and delivery systems.

Simply put, Gutenberg applied the ancient technique of the wine press to moveable metal letters.

📖 The evolution of early printing is summed up this way:

Around 1040, the first known movable type system was created in China by Bi Sheng out of baked clay. Metal movable type was first invented in Korea during the Goryeo Dynasty (around 1230). Neither movable type systems was widely used, one reason being the enormous Chinese character set.

Around 1450, in what is regarded as an independent invention, Johannes Gutenburg introduced movable type in Europe, along with innovations in casting the type based on a matrix and hand mold. Gutenberg was the first to create his type pieces from an alloy of lead, tin and antimony – the same components still used today.

Compared to woodblock printing, movable type page-setting was quicker and more durable. The metal type pieces were more durable and the lettering was more uniform, leading to typography and fonts. The high quality and relatively low price of the Gutenburg Bible (1455) established the superiority of movable type, and printing presses rapidly spread across Europe, leading up to the Renaissance, and later all around the world. Today, practically all movable type printing ultimately derives from Gutenberg's movable type printing, which is often regarded as the most important invention of the second millennium. [Information from www.Wikipedia.org]

Letterpress printing is a term for printing text with movable type, in which the raised surface of the type is inked and then pressed against a smooth substance to obtain an image in reverse. In addition to the direct impression of inked movable type onto paper or another receptive surface, the term letterpress can also refer to the direct impression of inked media such as zinc "cuts" (plates) onto a receptive surface.

Early Chinese woodblock printing used characters or images carved in relief from before 750AD, and this form of printing was widespread throughout Eurasia as a means of printing patterns on textiles. Printing of images, first on cloth, then from about 1400 on paper was practiced in Europe. In the 1400s, Johannes Gutenburg (among others) is credited with the invention of movable typr printing from individually-cast, reusable letters set together in a forme (frame). This had previously been invented in Asia, but the two inventions were probably not connected. He also invented a wooden printing-press where the type surface was inked and paper laid carefully on top by hand, then slid under a padded surface and pressure applied from above by a huge threaded screw. Later metal presses used a knuckle and lever arrangement instead of the screw, but the principle was the same.

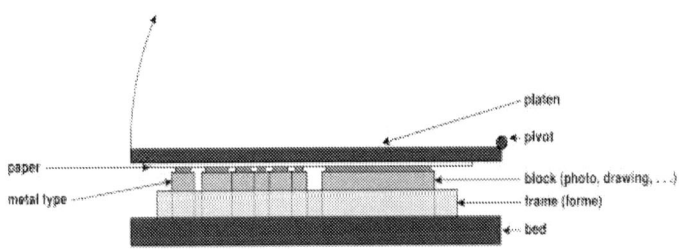

With the advent of industrial mechanization, the inking was carried out by rollers which would pass over the face of the type and move out of the way onto a separate ink-bed where they would pick up a fresh film of ink for the following sheet. Meanwhile a sheet of paper was slid against a hinged platen (see image) which was then rapidly pressed onto the type and swung back again to have the sheet removed and the next sheet inserted (during which operation the now freshly-inked rollers would run over the type again). In a fully-automated 20th Century press, the paper was fed and removed by vacuum sucker grips.

Rotary presses were used for high-speed work. In the oscillating press, the form slid under a drum around which each sheet of paper got wrapped for the impression, sliding back under the inking rollers while the paper was removed and a new sheet inserted. In a newspaper press, a papier-mâché mixture (flong) was used to make a mould of the entire forme of type, then dried and bent, and a curved metal plate cast against it. The plates were clipped to a rotating drum, and could thus print against a continuous reel of paper at the enormously high speeds required for overnight newspaper production.

As computerized typesetting and imaging replaced cast metal types, letterpress began to die out, as high-speed photographic imaging onto smooth flexible plates, known as offset litho, printing became more economical.

A small amount of high-quality art and hobby letterpress printing remains — fine letterpress work is crisper than offset litho because of its impression into the paper, giving greater visual definition to the type and artwork. Today, many of these small letterpress shops survive by printing fine editions of books or by printing upscale invitations and stationery. They are just as likely to use old printing methods as new, for instance by printing photopolymer plates (used in modern rotary letterpress) on restored 19th century presses.

The process requires a high degree of craftsmanship, but in the right hands, letterpress excels at fine typography. It is used by many small presses that produce fine handmade limited-edition books and artists' books. [Information from www.Wikipedia.org]

CALLING ALL AUTHORS—Valerie Connelly

Now, leap forward to 1997. This year marks the beginning of the high-speed, digital revolution in printing with the advent of Lightning Source, Inc., an offshoot of Ingram Book Company. Since the first books came off the presses to make the first three-hundred books at LSI, the marketplace has altered irrevocably. From the Lightning Source Website, here is the information in a nutshell:

📖 Lightning Source at www.lightningsource.com "is the leader in demand-driven book manufacturing and distribution solutions to the publishing industry. We are a customer-focused organization that manufactures superior quality books for publishers, in any quantity, and ships them all over the world.

📖 Our company was launched in 1997
📖 We are a subsidiary of Ingram Industries Inc.
📖 Our headquarters are located in LaVergne, Tennessee
📖 We have production facilities in both the US and UK
📖 We print over 1 million books every month and our average print run is 1.8 copies.
📖 Our digital library houses over 400,000+ titles
📖 We have manufactured over 33,000,000+ books to date
📖 We are partners with the leading book wholesalers and retailers in the book industry
📖 We are delighted to work with over 4300+ publishers —large and small. The concept of printing one book at a time, better known as Print On Demand, took hold for titles previously out of print, and for books produced for sale on the internet. Many printing firms have stepped into this realm, worldwide, allowing for global production of books as never before."

The battle royal between established commercial publishers and a new wave of POD publishers ensued, and has created true publishing freedom along with publishing chaos for writers and authors everywhere. The marketplace in the United States alone now struggles under a yearly explosion of 200,000 and more books published by self-publishers, small and medium-sized independent publishers, enormous author mills and commercial publishers (sometimes called traditional publishers).

The online bookstores such as Amazon.com, BarnesandNoble.com, Borders.com and the like market their books, which are now typically printed after they are sold, to a global market. Every publisher, whether a self-publisher or a mainstream firm, has a website with a bookstore, where the books are available to those who come to browse. Book clubs, philanthropic organizations, online specialty stores, writing services, writer's organizations, publisher groups, television infomercials and just about every imaginable outlet store from Wal-Mart to Costco and Sam's Club sells books where most of the books are printed before they are sold, or they are returns jobbed out for deep discount sale (for outlet stores in particular).

The initial financial risks involved with one at a time printing are minimal. The cost of the file upload service and the per book cost at the time of printing represent the only outlay required. Of course, the actual costs of editing, cover and interior layout and design, marketing and publicity add to this. But, at the bare bones of the work, print on demand eliminates the pre-press expenses of film, plates, lengthy proof corrections and re-casting of the film and plates. The time frame of bringing a finished book to production status is reduced from months to about ten working days, and faster if the firm has a smaller load to manage.

The absolute need to warehouse books is soon to be a thing of the past. This doesn't mean that books are no longer warehoused. They are. The lower per book cost of offset printing of books make the viability of first and second print runs of as few as a thousand to several million books attractive for books that have a demand in the marketplace. Distributors work with warehoused books, and wholesalers do as well. However, the virtual inventory is a reality for any book printed digitally.

For example, Ingram's iPage lists the hard copy and virtual inventory for each publisher, showing a virtual inventory of one hundred books for the digitally produced titles. A virtual inventory refers to the capacity of the printer to produce one hundred books in under forty-eight hours from order to shipping. The actual inventory may be one or two books ready for immediate shipping. Color books, such as illustrated children's books, take up to four working days, but this time frame is dropping fast. In 2005, printing color books required about ten working days.

The initial downside of digital printing in the marketplace was simply that if a book was not actually in a warehouse somewhere, it was technically out of print, or on back order. Bookstores will not order books that carry either status. So, the wholesalers devised the virtual inventory to correct this issue. And, since a digitally produced book will ship just as fast as a warehoused book, the virtual inventory makes the books available to the bookstore just as quickly as the actual hard copy inventory does.

The price differential of print cost per book is where digital printing still lags behind offset printing. In spite of the fast turnaround time, the per copy cost of a digitally printed book runs about 42% higher than an offset printed book. Of course, the cost of paper affects print costs, as do the kind of printers who quote the offset pricing. Print on demand books from LSI are all printed on 55 pound cream paper or 60 pound white paper.

There are as many offset print quotes as there are offset printers, and given some competition, a savvy publisher can bring down the print cost of offset printing even more. But, the outlay of several thousand to several tens of thousands of dollars to produce a print run is typically beyond the self-publisher, the small publisher, and those who believe the books they are publishing will not create the marketplace demand to support an offset print run.

The leading wholesalers and bookstores will list LSI printed books on in-store search computers and virtual inventories. However, the leading distributors require offset printed books and a hard copy inventory. Major booksellers such as Barnes and Noble and Borders can order in LSI books from the Bowker Books In Print virtual inventory listings, Ingram or Baker & Taylor virtual inventory listings. But, they are hard pressed to put LSI books on the shelves, except in a very limited way for a local author booksigning. Per book print cost drives the marketplace, and digitally printed books are still too expensive for widespread distribution where the demand must exist for the books to be put on the shelves.

Distributors sell books to bookstores, not wholesalers or printers. This is why the offset print run is still a requirement to get books on the shelves. Unfortunately, the self-publisher, the independent press, and the writers serviced by author mills and POD vanity firms are typically unaware of this circumstance, and once made aware of it, will back away from the bookstore market rather quickly. Even the groups and organizations that support the self-publisher and the small publisher, such as Publisher's

Marketing Association, Book Sense, SPAN, and many others, carry with them a strong bias toward offset printed books.

POD or one book at a time printing is perfect for the internet. The costs incurred with digital printing are not so great an issue for books sold direct from author or publisher to the consumer, as is the case for website direct sales.

For authors whose publishers sell their book on publisher websites, it is important to understand the difference in royalty structure required between the Amazon.com bookstore and the publisher's or author's own website. Amazon.com (and the other online bookstores) first takes the customary 55% wholesale discount off the top of the retail price, discounts the book about 30%, and sells it with a margin of 25%. So, to illustrate:

Consumer Retail price:	$19.95
Wholesale 55% discount:	$10.97
Amazon Purchase price:	$ 8.98
Sells at 30% off retail	$13.98
	$ 4.98 Amazon's Profit
Publisher Income:	$ 8.98
Print cost:	$ 4.92
Publisher net:	$ 4.06

Author royalty comes from the publisher net. If the author is a self-publisher, he gets all the revenue. If he has a publisher, then the percentage stipulated in his contract is what he will receive. The common industry author royalty is typically about eight percent. Some small presses have higher royalty rates and how much higher depends on the publisher's business model.

Also, the time required for the money to filter from Amazon (or any bookstore for that matter) back to the publisher is typically three to six months. The publisher may pay semi-annually or annually, depending on the way he gets paid by the industry sources he works with.

Sales on the publisher's website are far better for the author, though they may not be as plentiful.

For example:

Consumer Retail price:	$19.95
Print cost:	$ 4.92
Publisher net:	$ 15.03

Even with a 30% discount to compete with the Amazon discount, the results are much more advantageous on a website:

Consumer Retail price:	$19.95
Sells at 30% off retail	$13.98
Print cost:	$ 4.92
Publisher net:	$ 9.06

Shipping costs are paid by the consumer and are included in the sale to the publisher, covering those costs. The books are printed and sent directly from the printer to the consumer, so there is no fulfillment expense for website direct sales either.

Experience is truly the best teacher, and I learned all of this first-hand. The world is filled with hopeful, talented authors, most of whom are unprepared to become self-publishers. The background in the print industry that helps make a good publisher is usually not part of the common man's skill set.

CALLING ALL AUTHORS—Valerie Connelly

When I started Nightengale Press to become a self-publisher, I had worked in advertising as a copywriter, had worked with the first computer typesetters, had owned a letterpress print shop making custom greeting cards using artwork made from medieval block print techniques transferred to zincs and printed on antique crash print machines, and I was a computer graphic designer. I had been an educator for many years. I brought to my first books and authors a strong ability to design the books, understanding of the print industry, the personality to learn all there is to know about the publishing industry and provide education for my authors. Nightengale Press is truly author-centric and strives to support our authors fully and completely.

CHAPTER 9
The Publishing Revolution—Knowledge Is Power

Just get it down on paper, and then we'll see what to do with it.
—Maxwell Evarts Perkins, 1884-1947

Writers, who would be authors, work diligently on their manuscripts, and then one day, decide they are ready to find a publisher. The definition of what a publisher actually is has changed with the growth of high-speed, digital technology in printing. In the former world of publishing—before the advent of computer typesetting (1970's), desk-top publishing (late 1980's to mid 1990's), digital printing via print-on-demand high speed book binding (late 1990's to the present)—trying to get a book published was a lengthy and laborious process. In simplest terms, the sequence of sending query letters to agents and publishing firms, waiting long periods of time before receiving rejections, and finally quitting the search with frustration and failure as bed-fellows was common for most writers. For the comparatively few writers who succeeded in getting their books accepted for publication, whether with the aid of an agent or not, the publisher took control of the manuscript, produced the book, marketed the work and sent the author whatever royalty the book earned. The publisher was powerful and was driven largely by the bottom line requirements of the business.

The publisher worked with editors, layout designers, cover designers, printers, distributors and wholesalers. The author was a spectator to the creation of his book, and in the end, did whatever the publisher asked him to do in the promotional end of the job without much financial risk at all. Yes, great books were published. Yet, one must wonder how many great books never saw the light of day.

Since the late 1990's, there has been a powerful evolutionary shift from the old ways of printing books, a quantum leap forward in the publishing world, which has freed beleaguered writers languishing in the prison of obscurity. If the writer chooses to avail him or herself of the new and broader spectrum of book production, then it is safe to say gone are the days when writers had no control of their book's production and marketing.

The old ways still exist, and still govern the high-end realm of publishing, primarily because of the high costs associated with the old ways of producing books. But, as with the aristocracy in France just prior to the French Revolution, the rise of the publishing middle class has changed the publishing landscape forever, and the kings and queens of publishing royalty have had to sit up and take notice. Paupers still hunger for bread, but even they have a way to get their books made, and with creativity and perseverance can make a success of their work.

SELF-PUBLISHING—What it is and what it is not.

True Self-publishing boils down to these four things:

- **Control.** With self-publishing, the writer controls all aspects of the publishing process, from ISBNs and cover art to print style and pricing.

📖 **Revenue.** With self-publishing, the writer keeps all proceeds from sales.

📖 **Rights.** With self-publishing, all rights remain with the writer, who has full ownership of his/her books.

📖 **Risks.** With self-publishing, all the risks remain with the author/publisher, in particular the financial risks.

📖 **"Self-published" books are really of three types:**

Vanity and POD Presses (as discussed below) produce one type publisher who lets the author think he is his own publisher. The reality of the author's circumstance couldn't be farther from that impression. The author is not his own publisher with these firms.

The emerging class of independent self-publishers, authors who take on all the responsibilities of publishing a book properly. They establish an imprint, purchase their ISBN numbers from R.R. Bowker (ten minimum for $25 per ISBN) pay an independent editor ($350 to several thousand dollars), hire a cover designer ($500 and up) and book layout designer ($500 and up), and they send out review copies and news releases just like any other publisher. And still, these books are typically considered to be vanity books. Some may be motivated by the author's desire to publish at all cost, but more and more are properly produced and creatively marketed.

The self-publisher's ability or inability to take on the role of publisher varies from author to author. Some are overwhelmed by the whole production process, and when the shipment of books arrives, they store it in the garage or basement with a sense of bewilderment about what to do with all those books. But serious self-published authors pay for and work with publicists and marketing consultants, seek distribution deals, participate in bookstore mailings, put together sell sheets and fact sheets, and play the game by the rules. What they are unable to do, for the most part, is work with the power elite of publishing, because they don't circulate in that class, and some would say they don't need or want to.

A third category of self-publishers are those who already have a public speaking career and are selling books at the back of the room. They produce their books and sell them to a niche audience and so, don't need mainstream reviews, a bookstore presence, industry distribution and all the rest.

SMALL AND MEDIUM SIZED INDEPENDENT PUBLISHERS—How they are changing the publishing landscape.

Many smaller publishing houses choose to follow the "classical" design of the commercial publishing firm, paying small advances, taking all the financial risks and producing books pretty much the same way as the large houses do. These firms come and go quickly, simply because the dollars involved are many and the returns in publishing are few—until the firm is established and making substantial revenues from books sales. Large outlays of cash for investment in the authors, the costs of designing the books, the first print run and publicity can easily top $10,000. This is not for the feint of heart, especially if the firm publishes five to ten books a year. Some venture capital can be helpful, but is very difficult to attract. Why? Because publishing is a very risky business.

How Nightengale Press is different from all other publishers, large and small, Classical and POD.

I suppose you were expecting me to talk about my own press. I do not intend to seem self-serving here, but to illustrate how and why, as I developed Nightengale Press, I decided to invent a different publishing business model, more common to other kinds of businesses:

> To charge fairly for the work
> To pay the best royalties in the industry
> To provide a salable product
> To provide excellent support and education
> To provide opportunities to share publicity expenses
> To provide industry connectivity
> To put the needs of the authors first

Key elements to Nightengale Press's revolutionary business model are these:

We charge a fair and competitive fee for the time and expenses required to produce the author's book, the development and maintenance of the author's own Web site and at a level of professional standard the author could not achieve on his or her own as a self-publisher.

We also repay this fee to the author by paying a 100% royalty until his investment dollars are recouped through the sales of his book. Also, the author can purchase his books AT COST for the first 100 books for resale and speed up the time it takes to recoup his investment.

- 📖 **We pay the author a 50% royalty on the net proceeds** (retail – 55% of retail to Ingram – print cost), retaining 50% for the publisher from sales of the author's book in bricks and mortar bookstores, and online Web site sales other than through our own Web site. This royalty still equals or exceeds the average 8%-12% royalty of a commercial publisher pays on the gross receipts by 1% to 6%.

- 📖 **When the book sells on the author's Web site** or the Nightengale Press bookstore, the author splits the net 50/50 (retail – print cost) without the 55% cost to Ingram. This exceeds the commercial publisher's gross receipt percentage royalty by 33%.

- 📖 **If the author has reason to sell books in the back of the room,** he gets 70% of net ((retail – print cost + 30% for the publisher) which exceeds the commercial publisher's royalty by 400%.

- 📖 **Nightengale Press pays royalties on a regular six month schedule,** produces well-designed, edited books and helps the author promote his work through the PMA model of cooperative marketing, advertising and PR opportunities.

- 📖 **There is nothing confusing about what we offer the author.** Our authors win at all levels and their royalties never falls below the rate of the "classical" commercial publisher. Nightengale Press is in its fourth year, we have thirty-six authors with over fifty published and forthcoming titles among them, in mystery-thriller, sci-fi, romance, military non-fiction, medical non-fiction, fitness, inspirational non-fiction, children's educational, children's poetry, juvenile fiction, humorous short story, historical fiction, adventure, and living memoir genres. The roster of authors continues to grow, but we do not take every author that appears on our horizon, and we do work to promote every book to the extent the author will allow and participate in the work of promotion.

📖 **Pricing the book is dependent on page count,** how hot the topic of the book is and what promotional schedule is planned. Pricing is dependent on covering print costs, wholesaler and distributor percentages and still having a royalty for the author of at least $.50 per book through bookstores and other online stores than the author's Web site or Nightengale Press's bookstore. Our trade paperbacks average $15.95. The full color children's books average $16.95, more expensive, but not outrageously so.

📖 **Nightengale Press works hand in hand with stores** in the author's local realm. Some authors need help with this, and Nightengale Press works to get group and individual author signings in bookstores where several authors are clustered within a reasonable driving distance.

📖 **Nightengale Press offers trade distribution for selected titles** through BookWorld, a distributor that reaches 90% of the bookstore marketplace. These books will be printed offset in a print run of two thousand books and will still be available online as they currently are with the print on demand print option through LightningSource, Inc.

📖 **Nightengale Press books are available for order in bookstores nationwide** through Ingram, Baker & Taylor, Bowker's BooksInPrint and failing all of that, directly from the publisher. We stress the importance of creating demand to our authors, and we help them find the means to do so individually and collectively.

📖 **Nightengale Press pays standard distributor discounts and accepts bookstore returns.** This willingness to play by the traditional rules when necessary sets us apart from msot small publishers. We can get our books into bookstores for author signings, and with our new arrangement with BookWorld, we are opening the tradtional doors to shelving our books in stores as well.

📖 **We provide our authors the option** to have a full fledged comprehensive and attractive Web site devoted to them as individual authors and to their books. We also have featured titles on the bookstore and rotate these periodically so give all our authors exposure there as well, even those who do not have a Web site. But, let me say, only two of our authors do not have a Web site.

📖 **Our response time to emails is typically within two hours.** Everyone is very busy, and to sit all day working at email isn't practical, but setting a portion of time aside for that task, and multi-tasking is a way of life in a good publisher's world. We take calls and deal personally with our authors. We are truly invested in our authors' needs and desires, with all efforts made to communicate with them collectively, as individuals and on their behalf with whomever we can.

Nightengale Press consistently produces award-winning books and we have good opportunity to dispell the notions that swirl in the marketplace about a publisher that charges a fee. The reason there is an issue goes back to the dawn of "vainty publishing," where the publisher took a fee, produced books of sub-standard quality, charged high fees to the author, provided no makrketing, did not pay a royalty, and essentially left the author dangling in the wind. Old stereotypes die hard, and some new twists on the old "vanity press" model make life even harder for small presses who are embracing the new printing technologies. The term "POD publisher" is fraught with confusing and negative connotations. There are many reasons for this confusion.

I must stress that Print On Demand is a Printing Process. It is not a publishing standard.

The printer makes the book after the customer has paid for the product. It eliminates the need for warehousing. It levels the marketing playing field by eliminating waste and inefficiency. It takes the risky "betting on the horses" elements out of the publishing model, eliminates returns, and has opened the floodgate so far that over 200,000 books are published every year. Not all of these book are good books. Not all of them are bad books either. And, agents, reviewers, bookstore buyers, distributors, and the giants of commercial publishing cannot compete with items like instant payment to the publisher, nearly instant production and shipment to the customer, and the enormously fluid availability of books from talented, unknown authors.

LARGE SELF-PUBLISHING VANITY PRESSES—Publishing Firms to be Careful About.

The big three POD firms are Xlibris, Author House, and iUniverse in no particular order. Others to be aware of are Lulu, Publish America and BookSurge, once a POD printer, now trying to be all things to all people since Amazon acquired it in late 2004. There are many others, and you will find them all on the web.

Typically, three things happen within these firms:

- **There is little or no quality control** because anyone with a manuscript can get it made into book form "as is" for a relatively small charge.

- **The book covers are mass produced**, some even using templates for the author to make his own cover, which marks the books as amateur's work

- **The POD/Vanity firms provide little or no marketing assistance** to the author and openly count on the fact that authors rarely think about who besides friends and family would be interested in their books and how to reach those audiences.

Xlibris, Author House, and iUniverse books average 100 to 200 copies in sales, mostly purchased by the authors. While there have been some highly publicized successes, the average book from a POD service sells 150-175 copies, mostly to the authors themselves and to "pocket" markets surrounding them (friends, family, local retailers who can be persuaded to place an order. According to the chief executive of POD service iUniverse, quoted in the New York Times article mentioned above, 40% of iUniverse's books are sold directly to authors.)

The most recent online Fact Sheet for AuthorHouse, one of the largest and oldest of the POD services, reported 27,000 titles in print as of 2004, with total book sales of over 3 million. It sounds like a lot, but averages out to around 111 sales per title.

iUniverse's most recent Facts and Figures sheet reports that the company has published 22,265 titles through 2005, with sales of 3.7 million: an average of 166 sales per title. (Obviously some titles can boast better sales--but not many. As of 2004, according to an article in Publishers Weekly, only 83 iUniverse titles had sold more than 500 copies).

A 2003 Wall Street Journal article revealed similar stats for XLibris: 85% of its books had sold fewer than 200 copies, and only around 3%--or 352 in all--had sold more than 500 copies.

One of the most popular and cost-effective of the POD services, Lulu.com, is explicit about its business model. In a 2006 article in the Times UK, its founder identified the company's goal: "...to have a million authors selling 100 copies each, rather than 100 authors selling a million copies each." A Lulu.com bestseller is a book that sells more than 500 copies. There haven't been many of them.

Wholesalers and retailers don't buy these books because they are lower quality (poor design), non-returnable and higher priced.

Royalties in POD houses are based on net proceeds (after printing and shipping) with confusing royalty arrangements, some not paying any royalty at all to the author until 2000 books have been sold, which clearly doesn't happen very often.

A subcategory of Vanity presses are the Author Mills which masquerade as commercial publishers, but are actually POD firms. A glaring example of this business model is one firm which offers a $1 advance and a seven year contract leaving not much of a risk for them and a long ball and chain for the author.

As a first-time author, I had first-hand experience with one of these firms, and I wisely chose not to do business with them. They even maintained that their contract was negotiable. However, when I tested their willingness to negotiate, I asked that the advance be increased to $1000 and the contract duration be reduced to three years. They balked, sending me a terse email saying they could no longer consider my manuscript. Of course not. When put to the test of their "Commercial" bluff, they failed to live up to their own hype.

When in doubt, test the contract

Author Mills base their business model on author volume (selling small numbers of books from a very large number of authors) rather than on book volume—selling large numbers of books from a limited number of authors, as commercial publishers do. Some of these publishers' catalogues include thousands of authors, most of them first-timers. Author Mills don't usually charge fees, and often misleadingly present themselves as "traditional" publishers— a name invented by the owner of one firm to make it seem they were a commeercial publisher—but in practice they more closely resembled the POD-based publishing service providers, with the same open acceptance policies, high prices, bookseller-unfriendly business practices, and minimal marketing and distribution.

COMMERCIAL PUBLISHERS

Characterisics of the classical commercial publisher who focuses on selling large numbers of books from a limited number of authors.

Commercial publishers buy all rights, which simply means you no longer own your book in exchange for an advance and royalties ranging from around 8%-12%, sometimes higher, sometimes lower. However, in today's world, even the advance is becoming a rare commodity and is typically available only to known authors or personalities with "star power."

Royalties are usually paid annually after the accumulated amount is greater than the amount of the advance. If the accumulated amount does not reach or surpass the advance, then in some cases, the author is required to re-pay the shortfall amount.

In exchange for the author's willingness to surrender all rights to the publisher, the publisher then transforms the raw manuscript into a professionally edited and designed marketable product.

📖 **The publisher takes all the risk** and pays for a print run to produce copies of the book for distribution. The publisher negotiates with distributors to sell the book to stores, who then sell it to the consumer.

📖 **Commercial publishers take all rights and most of the profits** because they are taking all the risk.

It is the publisher's money funding the book as it goes from manuscript to finished product. There are some benefits to working with a commercial publisher.

If—and this is a big IF—your manuscript is accepted, there are no out-of-pocket costs. The publisher will do all the editing, formatting, design and printing involved in creating a book for the marketplace.

The commercial can reach a wider traditional market, in some cases, because of their "power elite" relationships.

If—and this is another big IF— you can negotiate a particularly good advance or commitment to marketing, it might be a better payoff for you than you could achieve using your own means.

In some circles, there is more prestige in having a commercial publisher's name on your book, but this prestige is decreasing due to the downsides to working with a commercial publisher.

The author surrenders all rights to the work and how it is eventually packaged and marketed. If the author doesn't like what the publisher is doing with the book, he has no recourse simply because he no longer owns it. Commercial publishers attract authors with the promise of marketing plans, but if you search online, you'll find that many commercially published authors become disillusioned with the marketing strategy and amount of resources the commercial publisher actually commits. Ironically, many authors end up marketing their own books because they are frustrated with the poor strategy and execution of the publisher.

However, the more common myths about being commercially published are debunked by reality. Authors whose books are produced by commercial publishers assume their book will actually be in all the bookstores. However, it is usually not the case. Most books published commercially do not appear in all bookstores, or even most of them. There is simply not enough shelf space.

Commercial publishers usually accept returns (buying back unsold copies from stores) and offer deeper wholesale discounts—making the books more tempting for bookstores to stock. This requirement is a reality in the publishing world, since without returns and at least 55% wholesale discounts, which nets the bookstore between 20% and 40% discounts from the retail price, bookstores will not purchase the books.

The reality is this: if those books don't sell—and sometimes the window of sales time is only six weeks— the returns will be taken out of the author's future royalties. And though it is rarely enforced, most commercial publishing contracts have a clause that allows the publisher to request that the author even pay back the advance if the book doesn't generate enough sales.

📖 TWO IMPORTANT PUBLISHING MISCONCEPTIONS

NUMBER ONE: No matter where you encounter a fee in the publishing process, this is a sign of a vanity operation.

📖 Let's take this statement apart. If true, then what about these facts?

📖 **Self-publishing requires the author to pay ALL fees** associated with making his book, and the author's skill at being a publisher is clearly an unknown. Does he have print industry background? Does he have graphic design skills and experience? Does he write professional press releases? Can he surmount the stigma of self-promotion? Does he have deep enough pockets to go it alone for PR, advertising, reviews, awards, and the like? Is a self-publisher a vanity publisher?

📖 **Author mills don't charge a fee,** but they charge exorbitant, per-book prices of the author and do nothing to promote to the trade, and the author doesn't own his ISBN. So, the author is on his own for PR and advertising, reviews, awards, and the like and yet, will not be taken seriously within the trade, since he doesn't own is ISBN. He is trapped in a circle from which he cannot break free.

📖 **True Vanity Presses make no bones about it,** they work for the fee, promise nothing and produce doubtful quality books, leaving the author swinging in the wind. They may mean well, and they do get books into print that would not be in print any other way. But the authors don't know that. They should.

📖NUMBER TWO: An advance, even of just a few hundred dollars, is a sign of a professional operation.

📖Let's take this statement apart. If true, then consider these ideas?

📖Why is the advance the benchmark of a professional operation?
Old habits die hard. Commercial publishers do not always pay an advance against future royalties, but will pay royalties as the books sell. What about the little known possibility that if the book doesn't sell the author may have to re-pay his advance to the publisher? You could be liable for the advance you have already spent, and end up owing the publisher your advance to come from your royalties, which may be neglibile, or from your back pocket.

📖MISCONCEPTION-BUSTING QUESTIONS to ask when researching publishers:

📖How long has the publisher been in business, and has it actually published any books? This is a no brainer, but every firm has to start out with less than a year's experience, and it does not necessarily mean they are going to publish bad books. It also doesn't mean they are going to publish good books.

📖Are the books professionally-produced and of good physical quality? Have they been edited? Bad writing, sloppy formatting, and large numbers of typos or grammatical errors indicate a less-than-professional operation.

There are all kinds of editors in the world, good ones and bad ones. Ultimately it is the author's and the publisher's responsibility to be sure the book is well written. Most independent publishers work diligently with their authors to make sure their books are well written, encouraging professional editing both on the developmental and the copyedit levels, as well as in-house correction until the book is as error-free as possible. Even so, errors do occur, even in the most highly touted publishing firms' books. Typically, every book will have a few minor errors.

Good physical quality and attractive covers are no guarantee that a publisher is legitimate, of course, but their absence does indicate a lack of professional expertise, and won't enhance your book's appeal.

"You cannot judge a book by its cover," is the old adage, but yes, actually you can judge a book by its cover. But what appeals to one publisher, might not appeal to another. And in a previous show about book covers, it was pointed out that there is no one correct way to design a cover. The cover is the first magnet that draws the browsing reader towards a book. It is important, but not the only thing to consider.

📖 **Is the pricing reasonable?** As noted, POD technology produces a book at a higher unit cost than offset, and prices can be correspondingly higher. On the other hand, you don't have to buy, warehouse and distribute hundreds or thousands of books to get that lower per-copy price. This is especially important for self-publishers and small publishing firms. This can be a substantial discouragement for readers—who wants to pay $30 for a trade-size paperback? This is vanity press pricing. A reputable POD-based publisher will make an effort to keep prices at least generally comparable to traditionally-printed trade paperbacks, which run between $12 and $18.

📖 **Does the publisher accept returns?** Again, this is a sign of a more professional operation, and gives the publisher a better chance of selling its books into stores.

The bottom line is relatively simple: Ingram and Baker & Taylor require a 55% discount to handle the books. Returnability is essential for bookstore placement and orderability. Anything less than playing by these rules for mainstream bookstores makes getting the books into a store impossible, or very, very hard. Everyone, self-publishers, small independent publishers and large publishers must play by these rules if their books are going to be available or stockable in bookstores. And Nightengale Press does play by these rules.

📖 **Is there bookstore presence?**
Not all independent publishers are able to get their books into stores, so lack of bookstore presence doesn't necessarily mean the publisher isn't reputable. If there is bookstore presence, however—even if it's only local availability—it's another indication that the publisher is actively marketing its titles.

Local placement of books on the shelves requires a demand. If the publisher in the local area can create that demand with the cooperation of his author, then the books will go on the shelves for at least a short while. We have done this again and again. Most commonly, this demand is created by the author's participation in signing events and getting coverage in the local media.

📖 **Can you order the publisher's books in a bricks-and-mortar bookstore?**
Even if a bookstore isn't willing to stock POD-produced books, it should at least be able to order them. Publishers whose

books can be obtained only from the publisher's Web site, or from online booksellers like Amazon, are further limiting already limited availability. Availability is the key thing that separates a reputable independent press from the vanity and author mill kinds of publishers.

📖 What is the focus of the publisher's Web site?

Is it designed to promote the publisher's publishing services, or to promote the publisher's books? A reputable publisher's marketing will be book-focused—it will publicize its authors, and try to attract readers.

Independent publishers should provide clear information about their publishing services, AND they should promote their authors and their authors' books on the site.

📖 Is the publisher forthcoming?

Will the publisher and his staff answer your questions promptly, fully, and without evasion? A publisher who refuses information, or scolds you for asking questions, is a publisher to avoid.

Communitcation is the hallmark of a good, independent publisher. This is the strength of a smaller firm over a larger one.

Maryglenn McCombs, a former publisher and now an independent book publicist in Nashville, Tennessee, explained that personal service defines the line between a good and a great publisher.

"Publishers, small medium and large often do work hard for their authors' books, but do not communicate with their authors effectively throughout the process. The deafening roar of silence that results leaves authors in the dark about where their book is, where the marketing is and where the results are. Author involvement is the key to good relations in this business, and without it, publishers can fall into the trap of perceiving their authors as 'difficult' when really all they want is knowledge."

Lee German, publisher and founder of Sylvan Dell Publishing, specializing in children's books, points out the need for the smaller firms to provide great service as the primary key to their success. Response time and communication is altered by the size of the firm, and in simple terms the authors feel more important with smaller publishers, be they conventional or non-conventional firms.

"I have had authors from major houses come to us because they wanted to feel like they mattered. We make a concerted effort to work as a team with our authors and illustrators before the contract is signed, during the making of the book, and as the marketing moves forward. We keep our authors in the know throughout the process of developing, making and marketing their books."

All in all, publishers need to remember that their authors are people, and not just ISBN numbers, book covers and sales records. The fact is, without our authors, we would not be publishers. So, as human beings in the business of making and marketing books written by sensitive, caring, creative people, we should keep the human, personal side of the business on the front burner. The resulting cooperation and hard work produced by the authors we serve then grows by leaps and bounds.

📖 CHECKLIST OF QUESTIONS 📖

If you answer "NO" more often and "YES," consider getting a publisher.

DO I WANT TO SELF-PUBLISH—SETTING UP MY OWN BUSINESS?

YES	NO	
___	___	Do I have the money to start up a business?
___	___	Do I have printing experience?
___	___	Do I have the personality to take risks?
___	___	Do I have the persistence and staying power I will need?
___	___	Do I want complete control of every aspect of creating my book?
___	___	Do I want to learn how to work with bookstores and vendors?
___	___	Do I want to manage all the financial issues of a small business?
___	___	Do I have contacts who can help me along the way?
___	___	Do I have marketing experience?
___	___	Do I have high enough computer skills to manage all the details?
___	___	Do I have graphic design experience?
___	___	Do I have sales savvy and experience?
___	___	Do I see a market for my book beyond my friends and family?
___	___	Do I want to research and develop a market for my book?
___	___	Do I have a fearless attitude?
___	___	Do I fear failure?
___	___	Do I have very good to excellent writing skills?
___	___	Do I have a sense of optimism about life?
___	___	Do I learn new ways of thinking quickly and easily?
___	___	Do I have a strong work ethic that will support long hours?
___	___	Do I see the details as well as the big picture?
___	___	Do I have good to very good internet skills?
___	___	Do I have patience?
___	___	Do I have a vision and a plan for carrying it our?
___	___	Do I know how to organize in order to be more efficient?
___	___	Do I have a support structure of family and friends?

CHAPTER 10
Reality Breaks the Mold—Setting Realistic Expectations

No matter how well you perform,
there's always somebody of intelligent opinion who thinks it's lousy.
—Laurence Olivier, Baron Olivier of Brighton, 1907-1989

Most authors, and I was guilty of this too—and I still am to a much lesser degree, because I am a believer that all our authors' books are going to be successful—but most authors typically have truly unrealistic expectations for the publishing, marketing and sales of their books. I'd like to point out that some of the most common misconceptions that you'll need to know about, and I hope you will take this the way I mean it: in the interest of creating some reality in your expectations. So, the following are some caution-filled ideas I'd like to present for new authors to ponder.

One of the things new authors looking for a publisher learn to believe, whether they hear it from their writer groups or read about it in online forums, is, that if you have to pay to get your book published or to have your book agented, then you are not dealing with a legitimate publisher or agent.

Well, the simple truth is that most first, second and third-time authors do pay to have their books published. It is just a matter of who do you pay and how much. Eighty percent of the books by major houses come through agents. In fact, many authors will pay thousands of dollars to a literary agent just to get their books read by a commercial publisher, fifteen and twenty percent in commissions if it is published and then pay tens of thousands of dollars for publicists and marketing firms. If an author is not prepared to fund this kind of effort, a traditional publisher is likely to turn a cold shoulder and not take the risk to promote an unknown author.

According to Publisher's Marketing Association, which works primarily with the independent publishing community, seventy-eight percent of all titles published come from small publishers and self-published authors. It is awfully hard to say that seventy-eight percent of all books published are not legitimate. A Borders manager I worked with told me that eighty percent of the books on the shelves in their store were from small and mid-sized publishers, leaving only twenty percent of the books from the big five publishing firms.

What is success?

Another question I hear fairly often from new authors is, "Isn't traditional publishing still the best way to become successful as an author?" My response is that one of the most important considerations an author can make is to take a good look and what your view of success actually is.

The Author's Guild points out that a successful fiction book sells five thousand copies, while a successful non-fiction book sells seventy-five hundred copies. Do these figures match up with what you think success is for your book and how it will sell?

According to Tom Wahl in his book "Publishing for Profit," the average royalty is only 10.7% of the net. Now, as the first time author of a fiction novel, let's say you were lucky enough to get the average royalty, with five thousand copies sold at $8.99, it is very likely the return for the author (after printing, shipping and returns) would be less than $1500. If you pay less than $1500 to both the literary agent and the publicist, you're not only a great author to get them to work for so little money, but you'd have to be a very shrewd business person as well. But, in reality, you will never pay only $1500 to an agent and a publicist. Think about this as you try to get a traditional publisher.

What about getting an agent?

Agenting has gone electronic, too.

Patrika Vaughn is a book agent, breaking the mold of book agenting in the twenty-first century. She used to be a regular literary agent, who gave it up because agenting had become a white elephant. I asked her what is the role of the electronic agent in publishing.

"Instead of the old-fashioned method of snail mail, bulky manuscripts, and all of the tedium involved with that and the months and months it takes for authors to get a reply when they submit to the publisher, I create web pages which are basically the book's proposal, then I search my database, find publishing companies that publish like-type books, contact the editor and essentially say, 'Hey, I think I have something that is right for your list.' Go take a look at___ and I give them the link. This lets them pre-qualify the manuscript in about two minutes. If they look at it, think it is interesting and would like to see the manuscript, of course, with the click of the mouse, they let me know this.

"They aren't stumbling over all sorts of manuscripts in their office, writing those polite rejection postcards and letters, and they love it because in two minutes, they're done. Authors love it, because they never hear about the ones who are not interested. And authors also love it because I can contact up to a hundred publishing houses at a time. There is no consideration here about whether or not they accept simultaneous submissions, because I am not yet submitting. Within a week or two, authors know which publishers are interested. We continue with the normal agenting tasks, including going through the contracts for the authors to make sure it is to their advantage.

"Because we are flooded with requests to represent, we have had to say we need to charge for the critique because our time is our income. There are still people out there who say, 'Stay away from anyone who wants to charge for representing you.' On the other hand, we can save the author so much time and pain because the results of the critique could be one of three things:

📖 Wow, this is great let us represent you please.
📖 It's a good concept and has a lot of promise, but it still needs work and here is what we recommend you do.
📖 Don't quit your day job. I say that gently when I have to say it. I don't encourage them just for the sake of pulling them in.

"I have even suggested specific courses that could help them improve their writing...I like to think of myself as the author's advocate and not a Simon Legree.

"Advantages to electronic agenting:
📖 Authors don't receive rejection slips.
📖 The speed of response is a terrific advantage. [Rejection notices] take forever to arrive because [the criteria] typically states that they respond to queries in six to eight weeks, respond

to manuscripts in three months and accept no simultaneous submissions...you bundle it up, put stamps on it, kiss it and send it off. After three months you contact the publisher with a gentle inquiry...and they hunt for it, and maybe they find it and maybe they don't. You've lost three months, postage, packaging and emotionally you've lost a lost of steam.

 📖 **In fact, sometimes on a critique I'll say,** 'I think this is excellent, it has a very specific but small niche market, I think you'll be better off self-publishing because a large publisher isn't going to be interested in such a narrow market. This is really a great book, but there is no publisher who will take it on because of its a limited market.'

 "When a book has a sustaining market, nowadays, big publishers do very well with certain types of books, but more and more small to mid-sized publishers are out there now, addressing the niche markets. This also makes life very difficult for authors because they don't know how to discover which publishers are appropriate for [their books].

 "The major publishers make a big splash with a new book if it is by an author who has a track record for sales. They'll put marketing money into it, but in six weeks to three months, it is replaced with something else...the strategy of the big publishers is: make one big splash and you're done."

 "ElitAgent.com cannot get listed with Literary Marketplace because we charge to read the manuscript and charge a flat fee to maintain the Web site. On the other hand, we don't get a commission once the book sells. The authors retain all the rights and they end up richer than with a standard literary agent. It costs authors a whole lot less to work with us. Fifteen percent is quite a chunk of what traditional agents get, and twenty percent commissions are becoming quite common.

"Very few of the large publishing houses will look at a manuscript unless it comes from an agent, though they will look at manuscripts we represent. Publishers love us, because we save them so much time. Editors in publishing houses don't edit anymore, they're all acquisition editors, and they leave it to the agent to sort the wheat from the chaff."

I commented, "I had an agent who charged nothing more than a postage fee, and he didn't notify me at all, and any attempt I made to contact him, I felt I was intruding on something very private. I lost faith in the process, and that experience was one of the reasons I formed Nightengale Press."

Patrika continued, "Because I'm a published author myself, I have so much empathy for authors. Every three months, even if there is no news, I contact them. I know they're just sitting there, hanging on, wondering if this is the day they're going get a contract...

"I won't send a manuscript out that I don't think is in publishable shape. I read every manuscript. I am happy to give the author feedback and recommend places where the author can get the work done. I can't even read a book without a mental blue pencil in my hand. I can't remember a book that didn't have at least one of two typos. Even the books from the big houses have typos. We provide contact to what is needed to be done to take the next step. But, I take on only ten books a year.

"Major publishers figure they're going to make a profit on only three out of ten books they publish. An author I know about had a book accepted for publication – one that was not considered one of those three -- and was offered a standard boilerplate contract. This author had no choice but to accept it, and sat back thinking the rest was all in the publisher's hands. There was next to nothing done for that book in terms of publicity. So the book fizzled. The author got a minimum advance on royalties for the first printing, and of course there was never anything beyond the first printing. He didn't know he should have been involved with the people in marketing and the cover design. The happy ending is that the publisher offered back the rights to his book; sold him the backlog of copies at a discount. He bought up the remainders and self-published a second edition, and gets steady on-going sales year after year."

Go to www.elitagent.com to learn more about Patrika Vaughn's services.

More About Fee-based Publishers

There are many fee-based publishers in the marketplace today. They have many different approaches to how they do business. The best advice I can give you is to read the contract in detail and see how it answers these questions:

- How long is the contract duration. More than three years is a red-flag
- Is the contract exclusive or non-exclusive? Non-exclusive is better.
- What happens if a large publisher wants to publish your book? Typically a co-publishing agreement is the best route to follow, since your publisher (or you, if you are a self-publisher) has invested in your book's development.
- Does the publisher offer a means for you to earn back your investment fee before he takes a percentage of the sales?
- Do you keep the rights to your book?
- What secondary rights are included in the contract?

- 📖 **Does the publisher perform all the work** that produces your book, the layout and design, editing, cover design, initial press releases, copyright acquisition, and if not, what extra costs do they charge for any of these services?
- 📖 **Most importantly, does the publisher pay a royalty** from the first book sold? At what percentage?
- 📖 **Do you get free books**, how many and how much must you pay to buy your own books?
- 📖 **How many books do you get at print cost plus shipping**, and after you exhaust that allowance, how much extra do you need to pay for your books?
- 📖 **Do they have a professional online presence** with a protected and secure bookstore?
- 📖 **Can you have your own Web site** through your publisher?
- 📖 **Do they offer industry marketing opportunities** such as tradeshows, print advertising, press releases, and referral to publicists? Some publishers offer postcards and business cards and call it a press kit. Be careful there. A press kit is created by getting reviews and news coverage over time—with the 'press' materials the author and the book attract.
- 📖 **Can your book be printed offset as well as digitally?**

Just because a publisher charges a fee should not mean that the publisher is less than professional. It should mean that the author and the publisher become a team to produce the best book possible. You can get excellent support and product from a fee-based publisher, and you may have much more input about how your book is made.

More Common Unrealistic Expectations

"My friends and teachers all say I'm a great writer and don't need an editor." I hear this often. My advice to every author: hire an editor and a proof-reader, and make sure they are both professionals to make your book the best it can be. So many authors skip this essential step, and their manuscripts are rejected because of it. Even when the book is ready for publication, get a professional to proof it again.

One of the questions I often hear from a new author when the book is published is, "I'd like to purchase 1,000 books, please." It is important not to buy too many books at first in spite of how excited you are to have it. Buy just enough to send as review copies and to selected friends or people who helped you write the book—and get them to point out any typos they find—and they will find some. Usually the first run has still got errors that need correction which is a fact of life in publishing. If you have bought a thousand books, they're all going to have those errors.

One the other hand, if you have a very reliable source of sales, purchasing a large quantity of books can pay off. One of our authors, Patti Jo Ruskin, had a village fair in her home where she had planned to launch her book, *My Damn Adventure*. When she ordered five hundred copies, I cautioned her about what can happen, but she insisted, and we had the books sent to the address in her home town. She sold them all over a period of two days. This was a great thing for Patti, and her book continued to sell well around the world, since she had a reliable source of contacts in places as far away as Guam who continued to buy her book for months after the launch.

Another thing I hear frequently is, "My book is on Amazon, but it has a ranking of 1,205,675. Why?" Just because your book is on Amazon.com and all the other .com bookstores, doesn't mean it will sell. I remember the feeling of pride I had when my books were first listed on Amazon. I thought, "Yay! My book is finally out there with every one else." That is just it! Your book is out there with everyone else. There are millions of titles on Amazon.com and nobody is going to find yours, unless they know what it is, which means you have to publicize it.

This is the single most common misconception new authors often have: "Why haven't you, dear publisher, placed my books in a Barnes and Noble store yet?" Bookstores will not carry your book unless there is demand for it. That is something authors need to understand. You can help to create this demand locally by getting your friends to ask for it in the store and order it. That may sound a little crazy, but it does help. No store manager buys an unknown book. They're not in the business of putting books on the shelves the think are going to sell. They put books out they know are going to sell. The sales force a distributor employs will help with this, but the book still needs to be saleable and create interest at the sales level before a distributor will agree to try to put it on the store shelves.

Another thing, that especially self-published authors need to know: your book must have an ISBN and be available through a major wholesaler like Ingram or Baker & Taylor, or a major distributor. At the very least it needs to be listed in Books In Print which is managed by R. R. Bowker, the cataloging firm who provides all the ISBN numbers in the United States. To buy ISBN numbers, you have to be registered as a publisher. If, as an author, you want to get just one ISBN for your book, it isn't going to be possible. The minimum purchase is ten ISBN numbers. Many self-published authors just skip this step, thinking it isn't going to matter. But matter it does. You cannot get your book into any bookstore without it. To get into a bookstore you must have demand and your book must be properly made for it to qualify for a bookstore to show any interest at all, even locally.

Sometimes I get this comment, especially from my fiction authors: "My book is the best mystery (fantasy, sci-fi) title ever written. Everyone will want to buy this!" Be realistic about your book's marketability. There are an awful lot of fiction books in the marketplace. Check to see what's already been written in your fiction genre or non-fiction topic area—this is very important, you need to know what your competition is.

I grant you this, there is always room for another title in any genre or subject, but if your book is not competitive, only your friends and family will buy it. Your book may never sell much outside your realm of influence, unless you do a lot to make sure it does—and this means you do most of the legwork and show up for the promotions you set up. Even though you think it will be a great movie, that's a dream world expectation, and the last step in a long line of events must occur first before any film is made out of a book.

"My publisher isn't willing to spend much of his money on promoting my book. And, he tells me I have to wait a couple of days for a reply to my emails. What is he doing?" You need to remember your publisher is your ally, not your enemy—he wants your books to sell and will help you accomplish this. Most publishers provide you cost-effective marketing opportunities, but you have to follow through. No one ever sold a lot of books without exposing their work through advertising one way or another. You need to be willing to jump on board. These deals will be the most cost effective ones you'll get. You are free to pursue any form of advertising you can, and you should find unique ways to promote your book. Authors who are proactive and develop a strategy of their own in addition to what the publisher offers do better all around than those authors who sit back and wait for the book to sell.

Remember your publisher works with many authors, and has a timeline and workflow to manage to keep everyone happy. If they don't reply to your emails instantly, understand your publisher is working. Avoid demanding instant gratification (your needs met right away) If you have something you need your publisher to do, give them time to do it. Try not to be strident (or pushy, whiney, accusative, angry, all of the above) in your communications. You and your publisher can become great friends, but you don't want to disappoint your publisher by becoming difficult to work with.

Another misconception is: "**I want my book on the shelves NOW! Right after it is print-ready.**" Let your publisher set your publication date well into the future, maybe as long as up to 6 months into the future. The street date is when the book can be sold earlier. The pub date is when it becomes a released and published item later. Why would you want to have a gap in time? Well, you'd like to have time to get reviews, enter award competitions, get radio and television interviews set up, submit articles for feature coverage in local papers and the like. These all help with spurring sales. Authors are anxious to get their book into print to the detriment of their sales. New authors often don't realize how long it takes to accomplish the proper publicity.

And, last but not least, I hear this one all the time. "**There is this publicist who says he can make me famous - for only $5000. Is this a good idea?**" Be very cautious before you hire a highly paid publicist. Do the footwork yourself and get help from your publisher.

There are excellent publicists who work for fair fees. However, there are also people in PR who promise the world and charge a small, medium or large fortune, and often little, if anything, comes from their work, except that the publicist make lots of money. Be suspicious of a PR firm that promises payment only upon successful placement—all too often this can explode in your face—with lots of placements in small time markets that produce no revenue for you, but you then get to pay the per insertion fees, which can mean thousands of dollars. And, you've got nothing back. Also, realize, in publicity, nothing is guaranteed. No one, not even the most successful publicists can force readers, viewers or listeners to purchase the book they have successfully placed in print or on television and radio for you. They have done their job by getting the reviews, the coverage and the exposure. It is up to the public to buy the book.

Think Caution, Caution, Caution when hiring paid advertising, and publicity. But, on the other hand, do move ahead with paid publicity, if you feel you can afford the expense and that the job will result in sales. Always work with your publisher, get into writer's groups, work with your networking groups, develop relationships with your local media and journalists. Typically, they are just a phone call or an email away. These are great ways to help market your book.

📖 REVIEW WHAT YOU HAVE LEARNED ABOUT PUBLISHING
Explain what misconceptions you had and how they changed reading this book

CALLING ALL AUTHORS—Valerie Connelly

CALLING ALL AUTHORS—Valerie Connelly

CALLING ALL AUTHORS—Valerie Connelly

CHAPTER 11
Press Releases & Better Press Coverage

And the trouble is, if you don't risk anything, you risk even more.
—Erika Jong, 1942 -

The manuscript is completed, uploaded and made print-ready. The publication date is set four to six months into the future. The publisher provides some free galleys to the author and to any publicist the author may be working with. These are used to generate publicity in the media, to garner book reviews, and to submit for awards. If you are doing your own pre-pub publicity, getting book reviews, submitting the book for awards, and writing press releases can present a challenge.

There are fine services online for getting reviews of new books. Some are free review services, some are for a fee. There are also the mainstream reviewers like Kirkus, the New York Times Book Reviews, Book Review sections in major newspapers nationwide, and sometimes even reviews in smaller hometown papers. There are reviewers who write for online magazines and print magazines. Getting to these people is hard work.

But, the starting place for all of these outlets is the press release. Without a professionally written, properly formatted press release, all the rest of your publicity is much harder to accomplish. In fact, every time something good happens for your book, you should write a press release.

Brian Jud has granted permission for me to present his Press Release Guide, which I have used successfully for years and earned the highest value ratings on www.prweb.com for those press releases.

I recommend you go to Brian's Web site at www.bookmarketingworks.com to learn many details of promoting books; join his newsletter as well to keep abreast of the newest trends in book marketing.

BENEFITS

The first step is to write five benefits readers will get from reading your book. This helps you focus on the purpose of your press release each time you write one and for each purpose you write one.

You should practice each variation of Headline, First Paragraph, Body Copy, and Final Paragraph for your book. Try them all, write several different press releases, if they fit your book. And, be sure to let some other people read them before you actually use them. If they are convinced by what you write, perhaps then, so will the media be convinced.

HEADLINES

There are two general categories of headlines that will intrigue your reader and build anticipation for your body text.

A direct headline uses one or more of the primary sales features of your book as the attention-getter (50 Easy Ways to Make More Money).

An indirect headline attempts only to stop the readers and get them to look past the headline (Do all vampires have fangs?).

1.1 News Headline

This is the most common method of direct selling. News headlines feature your title in the same manner as if it were a noteworthy item of timely interest. Simply select the outstanding benefit of your book (from the perspective of the reader's audience) and present it clearly and quickly: TV Violence: Shocking New Evidence.

Whenever a new book arrives on the market, you should announce that fact with a news headline (Announcing the First Book to ...). People are interested in announcements and these headlines have high readership. Similarly, you can begin your headline with words that have an announcement quality such as Introducing .... , Just Published..., Presenting the Latest ..., At Last ...

Headlines beginning with the words New and Now typically have the same effect. Combining these formulas can have a positive impact on the reader: Just Published. A New Book About an Amazing Way to Grow Hair.

Do not use this technique unless you really have a news story. Once hooked, readers will continue on, looking for additional facts. If you disappoint them they will stop reading and never trust your releases in the future. And do not use exclamation points for added emphasis. Let your statement stand alone on its news value.

1.2 Primary Benefit Headline

This is a simple statement of the most important benefit offered by the title: A Hassle-Free Vacation. Guaranteed. It is not necessary to be cute since a straightforward statement can be a powerful attraction. Some people choose to use the title of the book in the headline on the premise that it will result in higher recognition. Others elect to use a subhead to strengthen the headline, drawing the readers into the body copy where use of the title is widespread.

One of the most important benefits of a book in a competitive segment is good value. If your release is directed to retail stores, you might want to feature a reduced price or a special merchandising offer. The word free is always an attention getter.

Make your message clear and compelling by beginning your headline with the words How To... (How to End Money Worries or How to Get A Better Job), Why (Why Your Feet Hurt) or Which (Which of These Five Skin Troubles Would You Like to End?). These types of headlines are interesting and address the reader's major concern: "Will this be of interest to my readers, viewers or listeners?"

A technique that has been proven effective is to offer advice (Advice to a Young Woman Traveling to Europe). The word advice suggest that the readers will discover some useful information if they read the copy, the knowledge of which they in turn can pass on to their audiences.

1.3 Emotional Headline

A common approach is that of capitalizing directly upon the emotions of the readers: New Help for the Lost Children of Kosovo. Typically the headline has no direct-selling value, but simply makes an emotional appeal to involve the reader. This approach can be used well with testimonials. An emotional quote from a well-known person in your field can add credibility to your message (I was Going Broke Until Read ...).

An effective emotional headline tells the reader that you

understand his or her audience (For the Person who is 35 and Dissatisfied). Keep in mind that certain books lend themselves to emotional approaches, while others do not. Make sure your title and topic are conducive to this appeal or it will be looked upon as frivolous.

1.4 Gimmick Headline

It is not always necessary to take the sane, sound, common-sense approach to snagging attention. There are times when a light opening is appropriate, one in which there is no apparent relationship to the title or content of the book. However, it is important for credibility's sake that you make this connection eventually.

A gimmicky headline is most effective when your title has few important competitive advantages to shout as news or a direct benefit headline, and lacks the sales appeal of an emotional one. For instance, a gimmick headline addressed to librarians might declare: This Book is Two Years Overdue.

One intriguing technique is to offer a challenge (Can You Pass This Memory Test?). Another gimmick is to use a headline of only one word. This method is most successful if the single word is meaningful, selects the right audience and asks a question (Nerves? or Bashful?).

Your gimmick might reveal the unexpected. For example, most headlines urge some form of positive, immediate action. Therefore, a headline advising the reader not to buy something is an effective stopper (Don't Buy Car Insurance Until You Have Read All These Facts).

1.5 Curiosity Headline

This technique arouses curiosity about your book by, in most cases, asking a question: What Ever Happened to Sex Education? However, it could make a curious statement: Three Inches From Life.

Both curiosity and gimmick headlines are methods of indirect selling. If you are selling a title that fails to offer any attention-getting appeals, then you could try these techniques. However, it is generally better to use a logical, believable approach to the reader's interest through a straightforward presentation.

1.6 Directive Headline

This type of headline is most useful when you wish to get an immediate action from your reader. Directive headlines begin with words such as Go Now! or Call Today... and therefore are better used when addressing your ultimate customers. On the other hand, these tend to work well with broadcast media whose producers are looking for an immediate reaction, such as on a radio call-in show: You Can't Stop Drunk Drivers.

There is no absolute formula by which you can determine when and where to use directive headlines. However, they do get people to stop and read because they are direct, concise and forceful.

1.7 Hornblowing Headline

When you can be specific, do so. If your title has outstanding selling points, take advantage of them in your headlines. But if you can find no such appeals in the book you may find it advisable to lure the reader with a headline that speaks in general terms about the merits of it. These are called "hornblowing" headlines: The World's Most Definitive Book on...

This approach is useful in other circumstances, such as when your title compares favorably with competitive books but still lacks a unique point of difference. It may actually have some advantages that, for one reason or another, are not important enough to build an entire release around.

FIRST PARAGRAPH

Once you have hooked the reader with your headline, you must deliver on their expectations or they will stop reading immediately.

2.1 First Paragraph

Begin each release with the city and state of the release (Avon, CT.)

In one or two sentences, expand upon the headline and set the hook. Increase the reader's level of interest by succinctly stating the Five W's: who, what, where, when and why.

BODY COPY

Use the body of your press release to continue the momentum started with the first paragraph, and get the reader to take the action you recommend.

Body copy falls into a few well-defined categories, each used in accordance with the general format and theme of your headline. The style of copy you use in the body of your release must follow the pattern and pace established by your attention-getter. If you use a direct, factual headline, your body text will usually be most effective if it, too, is factual. Likewise, if you employ a gimmick headline your body copy should explain the connection to your book.

3.1 Straight-Line Copy

Here, the text begins immediately to develop the headline. This is the most frequently used type. It is like a white shirt, red tie and blue blazer--correct for almost any affair. It directly follows the headline and proceeds in a straight and orderly manner from beginning to end. It does not waste words, but starts to sell the benefits of your book immediately.

3.2 Narrative Copy

Narrative copy follows the headline with a story that logically leads into a discussion of your book. Your text sets up a situation prior to getting into your selling copy. This can be a dangerous style to use because you must construct an interesting story that will keep the readers involved long enough to make your point.

3.3 Institutional Copy

Institutional copy sells an idea, organization or service. In many cases this is narrative in style because you are not trying to sell the value of a specific book. You may be announcing your 10th year in business or a new service for your customers. Your copy must create confidence in the company that sells the books, not your books themselves. The difficulty is not to get so wrapped up in the traditions of your publishing firm that the copy becomes boastful and the you approach is entirely replaced by the we. This will quickly turn a reader off, especially if you use this style following a hornblowing headline.

3.4 Dialogue and Monologue Copy

Dialogue and monologue copy permits the person giving the endorsement in your headline to do the selling in his or her own words. The trick is to retain the attention-getting power of the testimonial and at the same time sound natural and convincing. One way to do this is to let your endorser do the complete selling job throughout, or by including a few additional supporting remarks in your own or others' words.

3.5 Gimmick Copy

Gimmick copy depends upon humor, poetry, foreign words, great exaggeration, gags and other devices to create selling power. This is rarely used because in most cases you are writing a press release to tell a straight, informative story.

FINAL PARAGRAPH

Close the press release with a call to action so the readers know what to do and how to do it.

Summarize the benefits they will receive by acting, and offer some incentive to get them to do something now. If they put the release aside for later action, the momentum will be lost and the likelihood of a favorable response reduced with time.

4.1 Call to action

Tell the readers what you want them to do now. Should they call for more information? Go to your Web site? Make sure you are clear about exactly what action you want them to take.

Go to www.bookmarketingworks.com for more information and to learn about Brian Jud's services.

📖 📖 📖

When you have practiced the art of writing the press release, test it at www.prfree.com. In their own words,

"P.R. Free offers customized distributions with assistance from our complementary branch - We offer distributions to the Web's top news Web sites and services such as Google News, Topix, News Blaze, Lycos News, Excite News, Yahoo! Search, Eworldwire, Associated Press, Reuters, UPI - even chief journalists in a specific geographic location.

"PR Free is the only free press release service backed by a true wire service, not just a company that uses email as its primary method of dissemination.

"PRFree through Eworldwire offers a complete suite of Video and Audio products. Eworldwire owns and operates its own studios for all of its Multimedia production, video and audio. We are the only wire service that actually does this ourselves."

You will need to create an account with them. Sadly, or not so sadly according to publicists, there are no longer any truly free press release categories, so they ask that subscribers invest some money.

Also, www.prweb.com provides even more comprehensive distribution, and in their own words, they are,

"The recognized leader in online news and press release distribution services for small and medium-sized businesses and for corporate communications. PRWeb pioneered Free Press Release Distribution and continues to set the standard for online news distribution."

While PRFree still allows free submissions, the least you can reasonably expect to spend is $30, which is an excellent value, and of course, you can add upgrade stars and "friends" to increase you standing on the pages. At PRWeb the fees are higher, starting at $40, with the best value at $80 per release. You can add stars and friends to increase your ranking. Google: free press release services for many more options.

The media scours these pages every day. There are people whose job it is to find the newest, most interesting items in the vast number of categories available. You will set a date for the distribution of your press release, you will see how many hits it gets and how often it is picked up by the media. You won't know who picked it up, however.

Your first press release will go out on the web, and you will find yourself on all the search engines these services use. This will help you hone your craft, because you may get suggestions for improvement from the service prior to the release and from the rank they assign to your press release. You will learn, you will grow and you will become skilled at writing press releases this way. And, because you can, you will save yourself a lot of money over time by doing this yourself. It takes commitment and time to write the press releases, but it pays off in visibility for your book and for you as an author. And you will get better and faster at doing this very important task the more you write press releases.

📖 Getting Better Press Coverage

Once you have practiced writing and perfecting your press releases, and honestly, you really can get good enough at this to reach the media your self, or become a great help to your publicist who will be very glad you can write the release that she would then only need to edit. The purpose of the press release is getting press coverage. But there is more to it than that, much more. I am going to quote liberally from Keys to Better Press Coverage, by Diane K. Danielson, CEO of DowntownWomensClub.com still refers people to her article as the information in it is even more relevant today than two years ago.

Diane explains in her article how she "increased her hit frequency and get quotes (and pictures) in hundreds of publications, including The Wall Street Journal, The New York Times, The Boston Globe, The Christian Science Monitor, and Health magazine through relevant, witty, and helpful responses to queries from writers who were looking for the kind of material that she had.

"ProfNet (www.profnet.com) and similar services, which disseminate journalists' requests for information via email to thousands of experts and PR agents. I do my own publicity, using www.prleads.com to sort leads, so that I receive only those queries that relate to my book and my business. ProfNet costs $500 to $3,000/year, depending on your company status and desired sorting options. With flexible sorting functions, PRLeads currently costs $99/month for individuals.

"Staff reporters and freelancers...and most journalists don't even bother culling through their lists of contacts, let alone press releases, when they start work on a piece. (That expensive press kit you sent? It hit the circular file.)

📖 Diane's Rules for Responding

Originally developed as a bridge between PR professionals and writers, ProfNet also helps self-promoters. How can you take advantage? By recognizing two principles of responding to writers' queries:

(1) writers are never just working on a single story

(2) the easier you make a writer's job, the more likely it is that the writer will use you as a resource.

These five tips will help you avoid the automatic 'delete' button when you respond to a writer's query by email. Follow all instructions. [And honor these] five basic instructions [which] appear in almost every query.

- 📖 **No phone calls.** This really means "no phone calls." Unexpected calls are invasive and disruptive. They're also less efficient and harder to organize than emails. Any writer who wants to speak with you by phone will schedule an interview.
- 📖 **Name that query.** Put the exact query title in the subject line of your response. This helps writers, especially those working on multiple articles, organize their emails. Some writers even use Autosort, so that if you don't include the keyword, your email could be labeled as spam. I often put not only the title but a couple of words so that writers can easily find my response when they go back and cull through the group. For example, "Vacation Email Overload article–ruined trip to France."

📖 **Meet all expert qualifications.** Sometimes the writer needs only experts with a certain background or in a specific city. If you do not meet those qualifications, it doesn't matter if you have the best comment; the writer will not use it, and you'll be wasting everybody's time by sending it.

📖 **Do not send attachments.** Downloading is time consuming, and no one should ever download anything from an unknown source.

📖 **Deadlines are deadlines.** Most are not arbitrary, nor are they set by the writer. Emails sent after deadlines are useless. Most writers receive hundreds of emails and don't want unnecessary ones.

📖 **Answer the question asked.** Do not ask if the publication might consider a completely different article. Freelancers and even staff writers have no control over other articles in a publication. That's an editor's job. However, emailing a response to a writer's query that suggests a slightly different angle to a story can sometimes be helpful. For example, for parenting articles, Diane often writes: 'Have you considered the single parent's point of view, which is...'"

📖 **Diane then goes on to list three additional points that help you survive the delete button:**

📖 **Give them specific information they will need.** ... [so a writer doesn't] hit 'delete...'

📖 **Offer something original.** Writers are looking for new takes on what is often the same old subject...

📖 **Be a reliable, believable, and credible source.** While you can stretch your realm of expertise, step back and put yourself in the readers' shoes before you go too far.

📖 **How do you make it into print?** Here are five more ideas from Diane for fine-tuning your responses.

📖 **Quotable quips.** Respondents who can convey an original idea in a couple of well-written sentences in an email make life really easy for a writer. [Diane does] this by writing at least one sentence that could be a lead-in, a teaser, or a pull-quote.

📖 **Early responses.** Some writers might wait until close to deadline to review all responses together. However, if you get yours in early, they may read and be influenced by your thoughts.

📖 **Tips and lists.** Tips and lists are popular with writers, since bulleted lists can be scanned quickly, and a writer can pull a few tips from a variety of responses. Also, many articles use shorter, related articles or lists as sidebars.

📖 **Accurate identification.** In your email, say exactly how you would like to be identified and include any links to Web sites that would help a writer with fact-checking, by including all identity and contact information in the signature line.

📖 **Review copies.** Include a line offering a review copy if they're interested. Don't push it; just give the writer the opportunity to request one...Writers may want to see your book, and even if they can't use it this time, they might find a way to work with you in the future.

Finally, here are two don'ts so you won't ruin your chances of being quoted after you've survived two rounds of the delete button:

- 📖 **Don't badger writers.** A writer will use your quote if it works for a given piece. Calling or emailing journalists and asking whether they've read your email will not change that, although if you annoy them enough, they might decide not even to consider you. If a writer indicates that a quote from you will be included in an article, ask when it will run and take the initiative to find the story yourself. And don't forget: an editor might cut your quote to meet space requirements, and the writer has no control over that.
- 📖 **Don't give writers anything but your own original ideas.** It's not just your reputation at stake, but also the reputation of the writer, the writer's editor, and the publication.

Writing of any sort becomes collaborative along the path to publication. The secret to increasing your press coverage is to recognize how the process works for journalists and to become an invaluable resource for them. Remember, it's not about you; it's about being a part of an interesting story. The rewards, however, are all yours for the keeping."

Go to www.DowntownWomensClub.com for more information about Diane K. Danielson's services.

I have worked with a variety of journalists, publicists and writers who helped me provide needed press coverage over the years I worked as a singer/songwriter, as an educator, and now as an author and publisher. I consider making contacts and keeping those doors open a very important part of the process of promoting whatever you are doing.

As an educator, when I was traveling with my students on the summer immersion study/travel seminars I had developed for my non-profit organization Overseas Alliance, we met with then French President François Mitterrand at the Elysée Palace and were honored guests at the during the Bastille Day celebrations in Paris. This made the news in Chicago, in the suburbs and in Paris and all over Normandy, where we had our family homestay portion of the program. I did all my own PR for these trips, and the schools I taught for, as well as the towns I visited in France with my students, gained higher visibility because of my efforts. They liked that, and it helped keep the program growing for five years. Over eighty American high school students met the President of France. That was a good thing.

Later, when I was making my living in music, it became very clear that the work of my publicist was essential to my getting more work as a singer. We worked in tandem, and she managed to get me into all the major Chicago papers and most of the local dailies when I was performing in the city clubs. This kept people coming to my appearances, which made the club owners happy, and so I kept working.

Then, as a first time author, with lots of ideas and not much budget, I developed a following for my first novel by providing the 'features' writers at the local papers full articles to use that opened the front pages of their Business and Community sections to my story.

Now as a publisher, with a growing business and nearly forty authors to promote, some do find their own PR firms, while others rely on me to provide their press releases and keep up with their events. It is a valuable skill, and I encourage all authors to develop the ability to write great press releases using Brian Jud's superior format for press releases and get the press coverage they need by following Diane Danielson's advice on opening doors with journalists and freelance writers.

PRACTICE MAKES PERFECT
Practice Writing the Elements of a Press Release Here.
Then move on to writing your first press release on your computer.
This skill becomes an ART. You must practice.

In the following exercise, you will write in this book. What you write will be more like notes, than a finished press release. But, you are embarking on a means to providing yourself coverage and exposure. You will find yourself on the web with a simple Google of your name. Your press releases stay out there forever. You build a presence that will bring credibility to you and your book.

📖 **BENEFITS**—Write 5 benefits about your book
1)_____
2)_____
3)_____
4)_____
5)_____

📖 **HEADLINES**—Write each kind of headline for your book

   1.1 News Headline_____
_____

   1.2 Primary Benefit Headline_____
_____

   1.3 Emotional Headline_____
_____

   1.4 Gimmick Headline_____
_____

   1.5 Curiosity Headline_____
_____

   1.6 Directive Headline_____
_____

   1.7 Hornblowing Headline_____
_____

📖 **FIRST PARAGRAPH**
   2.1 First Paragraph

_____
_____
_____

📖 BODY COPY
3.1 Straight-Line Copy

3.2 Narrative Copy

3.3 Institutional Copy

3.4 Dialogue and Monologue Copy

3.5 Gimmick Copy

📖 FINAL PARAGRAPH
4.1 Call to action

Now that you've practiced this, take these notes to your computer, and shuffle them into five or six different kinds of press releases. Expand on your body copy, if necessary. Re-word your headlines and tighten your first and final paragraphs. When you have completed this exercise, test your press releases on PRfree.com and see what happens. Get your ratings, and see who picks it up. Then take the best one and put it out on PRweb.com. Pay your $40 to $80 to see what happens there. The ratings are excellent, and the stats you get are impressive. This process may take you two or three weeks to do well, but the skill you gain will be invaluable, and it will save you a lot of money in PR fees to pay someone to write press releases for you.

NOTES:

CHAPTER 12
The Essentials of the Internet

The shortest and best way to make your fortune is to let people see clearly that it is in their interests to promote yours.
—Jean de la Bruyère, 1645-1695

Authors often forget that the business of writing a book is just that: a business. Once written, the goal is to sell the book to as many people as possible for as long a time period as possible. The all time best sellers listed in the first chapter are not only selling today, but they were re-issued, many of them, as annual editions, and re-issued again and again. When the times changed, the books changed. From the original Latin version, the Bible then was issued in English in the King James Version, and in modern times, it has been translated into several "modern" English versions and into every written language on the planet. The Bible has sold more than six billion copies since 1451—five hundred and fifty-six years of sales.

The means to letting the public know about books has changed drastically as well. Certainly, in the early years, those who read were only among the educated or theological elite. The man in the street was illiterate. But, if one counts the last hundred and fifty years or so as the time period when books became available to more or less everyone who could read, and more and more people were included in that group, then it becomes clear that the task of selling books had to evolve along with demand and advances in technology. The printing press did make it possible to bring books out of the cloister and into the marketplace of the greater masses. But as soon as the Industrial Revolution automated production, transportation of goods on sailing ships gave way to steam ships, and ever faster trains brought books from the ports across the continents at faster and faster rates. When airplanes evolved into carriers, then books flew to even more destinations worldwide. Publishers, printers, wholesalers, and distributors set up complex systems for printing, warehousing, selling and transporting books.

One-book-at-a-time digital printing first appeared in the United States in 1997 at Lightning Source, Inc., a subsidiary of Ingram Book Company, in Tennessee. Today, there are few print houses that do not offer some kind of digital printing. Even the process of offset printing is directly impacted by the way the files are now made on computers and digitally transferred to film or plate. Computers have made it even easier and faster to manage and catalog the vast quantities of books and the increasing outlets where books were sold. 11-digit ISBN barcoding systems have expanded into 13-digit EAN barcoding systems to accommodate the explosion.

However, nothing has revolutionized how books (and just about everything else) are sold more than the Internet. Millions of titles are available to billions of people at the click of a mouse. Digital printing makes books available faster than ever before and simplifies the process as well. Enormous warehouses filled with books waiting to be sold are becoming a thing of the past, replaced by virtual warehouses where the books are listed as print-ready and show a virtual inventory so bookstores can order them. Today, when you order a book on the internet, more often than not, it is printed after you have paid for it and sent to you within forty-eight to seventy-two hours. Warehouses do still exist for the offset printed books that still ship to book stores, but I truly believe their days are numbered.

Think about it: the Internet Revolution is barely fifteen years old. Speed is of the essence in production and shipping. Amazon and Google, whether you like it or not, have changed how everyone does business. Every major book store chain has an online store. Publishers have online bookstores. Self-published authors have online bookstores. Everyone who has a business has or should have a website with an online store. There is nothing you cannot buy on the internet. For better or for worse, in fifteen short years we have expanded the marketplace and shrink-wrapped the world which we ship overnight to anywhere on the plant. It is pretty incredible.

Now, imagine the world in ten more years. Will bookstores be able to wait for books to ship from the warehouse? Or will they prefer to print the books in the store as the customers request them? Technology is already developed for exactly that. Will customers even want to walk into a book store? Well, with all the gimmicks book stores are using to draw customers through the doors, one must think that the job of getting the book-buying public to leave home and drive to the mall to go to the book store is becoming harder and harder. Without the café, the special deals days, and the hyped up releases of the mega-blockbusters such as Harry Potter, won't people simply choose to just "buy it online?"

And, what about eBooks. They aren't as cuddly as paper books, but they are printable right at home. Back in the late 1990's, Stephen King tried to sell a book as an eBook, for a dollar per chapter to have the right to download and print one copy of that week's or that month's release. It fizzled, and he continued writing for the printed book world. He was ahead of the curve, and I'd bet in another ten years, this will be a great way to sell books.

Yet, there are plenty of reasons to offer eBooks as giveaways, or a means to selling documents for the use of the individual, when the visual impact of a cover or the tactile 'feel' of the printed page makes no difference to the consumer. In addition, there are now eBook readers that make it possible to carry the eBook with you. Personally, I'd wonder why someone would want to carry a gadget, when a printed book will do. But, in the techno-gadget world of cell phones that let you play games and watch movies, let you work on a computer and allow you to communicate on the internet in addition to actually talking with someone, I'd wager the eBook will find its market.

The website: as essential as breathing

I remember thinking about developing a website in the mid-1990's when I owned a boutique print-shop. I wasn't sure the expense would bring in the business I was looking for to sell the custom-made greeting cards I had developed for small and medium sized businesses in the Chicago market. Looking back now, if I had been willing to risk setting up a website, I'd very likely still be making custom greeting cards, selling them on the web, and I probably would have developed an online eCard system. Well, live and learn.

You absolutely must have a website.

As an author, whether you are self-published or have a publisher, a website is a key ingredient to your ability to sell your books. It gives you a place to attract customers, and a place to make the most of your book. You will need to have one developed for your book. Many self-published authors make their own sites, to varying degrees of professionalism. But, Yahoo SiteBuilder is available on www.yahoo.com through their webhosting and merchant services, and provides just about everything the do-it-yourself webmaster needs, including a way to have a merchant account with a store where your customers can use credit cards safely. With a relatively basic understanding of computers (and I don't mean writing code, just a familiarity as a user) nearly anyone can create a useable and attractive website. One cautionary word of advice, however: web-mastering takes a lot of time and attention. So, if you don't like spending your evenings and weekends updating your website, tracking orders, and handling the details, perhaps you should find a webmaster to do the work for you.

If you have a publisher, he should provide a subdomain for each of his authors, or at the very least, a comprehensive author's page where your bio, an excerpt from your book, and interesting information about you and your book is contained for visitors to the site. There should be a buy function that allows visitors to purchase your book easily and safely from your site.

Ezines, E-newsletters and Blogs are great networking tools, even for the Internet novice.

You are a writer, and the advent of ezines, e-newsletter, e-articles and blogs will allow you to keep your skills sharp. Not only can you benefit from the array of linkable resources these internet forums provide, but you can expand your own market for your book by getting involved in the unending cycle of chatter. It is amazing how fast you can build a network through judicious use of the blog.

Blogging Tips and Tricks from the Gray Dog (www.thegraydog.org) The following is a transcription of the Gray Dog's informative appearance on Calling All Authors, December 28, 2006. The Gray Dog uses his canine persona to conduct interviews of political personalities, and the humor that engenders peaks the interest of lots of readers each day. The Gray Dog also creates videos to make fun of those who would hack his site, to generate emotion, and to comment on the world events.

"Hit the nerve, touch someone and generate interest and to avoid getting discouraged when no one is reading what you write. Your blog is 'home' where you can discuss local and personal interests that may not work as well for a group blog.

"Bloggers express opinions, and are not held to journalistic standards, but the widespread use of blogs by all major newspapers, television and radio stations and columnists have validated the pressure the blogisphere has placed on the national and world media to jump into this fast-paced internet realm. The credibility of the bloggers who caught the mainstream media passing off false information as true, some have become huge entities similar to a major newpapers with high advertising sales, different departments with fact checkers, and high credibility, as a result.

📖 Blogging is broken into two categories: linkers and thinkers

"Thinkers are the people who write and usually write opinion, and linkers are those people who start a blog to link to other stories, to make their site a composite location to find current and recent articles.

"Forums are interactive communities, more like a bulletin board with topical areas that are of interest and those who visit read comments and comment back. It is almost like a multi-threaded IM which takes up a lot of time, but causes people to think and to become informed.

📖 How to begin a blog:

- 📖 Go to Blogger at www.blogger.com to create a free blog in fifteen minutes by taking four quick steps in their system.
- 📖 You can move up to www.Typepad.com which provides internet active software, with a low monthly fee, and it is a great way to break into blogging.
- 📖 You can then move up to having your own webhosting service and use the WordPress platform with all the bells and whistles a blogger could need. Go to www.wordpress.com to download the free software they offer on their site, but you must install it at your own webhost service. You need to be able to use html and php programming languages, with a lot of computer literacy to use software of this kind.

📖 Elements of a good Blog:

- 📖 The writing needs to be of high quality and consistent. You need to have something to say, say it well and with some entertainment value.

📖 **Deleting blogs** the day after you write a blog is a no-no. It eliminates your credibility.

📖 **Spelling, grammar and coherency are important** to be able to argue with logic. Bloggers who can't really argue with your logical position will crucify you for grammar and spelling errors to try to prove that what you had to say has no merit.

📖 **Have someone proof your work** before you actually post it, hopefully somebody who is literate. In particular, punctuation is essential.

📖 **You must write on a regular basis** to maintain a readership, with posts almost daily, you will lose your readers.

📖 **People on the internet are impatient**, may not even hit the scroll button, so your post should fit on the page, be short and hook-y.

📖 **Site meter shows you who hits your first page**, or go on to other pages and spend fifteen or twenty minutes looking at your blog.

📖 **Blogging takes time, commitment and networking.** It can become an all-consuming passion competing for your attention and time. In business, the way you keep score is with dollars. In blogging, the way you keep score with links and hits. Links are the bread and butter and the backbone of becoming a successful blog. You must find sites that link to your site to build your site's ranking on the major search engines like Google, Yahoo and MSN.

📖 **Quick and easy does not work.** Do not subscribe to some search engine submission site that promises to get you a high ranking. What you will get from them are thousands of SPAM emails and SPAM comments at your blog site.

- **Go searching at blogs that are similar to yours.** Go find people who have eight or ten people linking to them. Drop a comment at their site or email them about exchanging links.
- **As you try to move up** to larger blogs with considerable readership there are several ways to attack the problem of getting linked to them.
- **There are trackbacks and pingbacks.** Go to a blog, read an article, perhaps write an article and then drop a comment and use the trackback or pingback feature to link your site and an article you have written that compliments their article.
- **Drop a comment and give a link that leads to your site.** Get involved and interactive in forums in your area of interest. This is easier, and you can start discussions with people. As they get to know you, they'll come to your blog.
- **Etiquette for dropping links.** If you are directing the reader to a link in a post or a blog, administrators will usually allow that. You shouldn't just tell people to come to your blog instead of the one where you found them.
- **This is hard work,** it takes time, see what others are doing, get involved, get interactive, leave comments and ask for comments.
- **Serious, established bloggers** make finding new forums and posting something part of their daily routine. Others blog in fits and starts.
- **A primary key to getting people** to come to your blog, is to have a good catchy title.

📖 Simple steps

📖 Register your blogsite at www.technorati.com largest index of bloggers. Everytime you write a new post, it is indexed and listed on this site. It has a broad spectrum of topics from politics to baking. Any topic you can think of has a blogging community.

📖 Google has a page calls zeitgeist at www.google.com/press/zeitgeist where you can find the most searched query terms for the week. This a good way to find topics that are hot in your area of interest, you can tailor your article about it. This will bring your site good threading through Google.

📖 Use Technorati tags as keywords in your blog and in your article title to draw Google hits to your article. Go to technorati.com to see what people are looking for and put the hot topics into your title. This is the marketing part of blogging."

📖 📖 📖

📖 Ezines—Use Articles to Boost Book Sales

Eric Gruber is an award-winning public relations practitioner, and article marketing is one of his specialties. He offers free consultations on increasing book sales by using Internet marketing strategies. Email eric@prleads.com or go to www.articlemarketingexperts.com to learn more.

Eric titles an article in the November 2006 PMA Independent *"Use Articles to Boost Book Sales,"* stating his premise that article marketing can contribute significantly to a strong, multifaceted marketing and sales plan. He then goes on to provide five steps everyone should include in an effective article-marketing program in your marketing plan.

Step 1. Target your audience via e-zines and Web sites that make a difference

"You need to find sites with high traffic and e-zines with sizable readerships; but more importantly, you want to focus on sites and e-zines in your specific niche that have strong emotional connections to their audiences….plenty of e-zine directories—like BestEzines.com—can guide you.

"And don't forget to check sites for print magazines within your niche. More and more print-on-paper publications are looking for fresh content for their sites that will drive traffic up and eventually sell more print copies. Articles published on sites such as those of Entrepreneur Magazine (www.entrepreneur.com) and Mothering Magazine (www.mothering.com) can generate a good deal of exposure and build credibility.

Step 2. Create an article that will grab your targeted readers

"One of the most important parts of any article is the title. Remember, the first three or four words of the title have the most weight with search engines, and the title's job is to get people to actually read the article.

"…Articles that get the best results are the ones with distinctive, high-quality content that solve at least one part of a problem. But since you want to turn readers into buyers, don't provide all the answers in your article. Instead, entice people with some of the "how" and top that off with why it's important.

Step 3. Turn readers into prospects with a strong call for action and an offer they can't refuse

"...To create your Unique Selling Proposition, chisel excess information from your first drafts of copy and refine the remaining golden nuggets into gleaming insights. Hammer them into logical sequence. Fasten them to reader benefits. Then polish and polish it...until it [is] more tempting to click and go to your Web site than to skip out.

"A free bonus offer will make it even more tempting for readers to click to your Web site. You can offer a sneak preview of your book, a free e-zine subscription, or a free special report that further enhances your credibility as the expert.

Step 4. Arrange to take readers to a squeeze page (sometimes called a landing page)

"Think of your article as a sales funnel. The title, content, and bio box and the link you provide should all flow right into each other. ... include a link to a squeeze page within your site that is designed to convince people to buy the book or subscribe to a related newsletter.

Step 5. Submit your article and build your links and traffic

"As you're working through [the tiring and tedious task of submitting your articles], remember the light at the end of the tunnel. By using these article-marketing strategies, you can build a steady stream of ready-to-buy visitors, and substantially increase your book sales."

Blogging, writing articles for e-zines, e-newsletters and e-magazines is a far better route to real connectivity to others in your area of interest. One last comment, if you have skills or knowledge that qualify you as an expert, then one of the best places to build a following is at www.ezinearticles.com. This is a tremendously well organized site, with a willingness to classify experts according to the validity of their articles. You need to follow their guidelines closely, and they will contact you to help you get it right if you don't. Another great place to market your book and post articles is at the Author's Den, www.authorsden.com. I use them both, and recommend them for all authors to develop a presence on the web beyond their own website or blog.

NEWSLETTERS

Francine Silverman uses Mailer-Mailer list manager (www.mailermailer.com) to handle the emailing of her newsletters. Another good service is Constant Contact (www.constantcontact.com) used by the National Association of Women Writers (www.naww.org). Francine researched newsletters for authors, and found that there was nothing available for them. So she devised a list of questions and asked for answers. She garnered ten subscribers at first. But because the newsletter is written by the subscribers who submit their ideas and successes, they in turn inform and inspire other authors to try what has already worked for someone else. Her newsletter quickly grew to over a thousand subscribers who contribute to the interactive format, changing the emphasis from blurbs and announcements to how-to tips from authors. It's alive. I asked her to tell her favorite success story.

"I love the story of one author I have, I think he's a suspense writer. When he goes to booksignings, he plants his wife at the front door, and when somebody walks in, she says to them,

"Do you read suspense?" And if they say, 'Yes,' she takes them by the hand and leads them to the table where her husband is standing...make sure you have a gimmick when you do a booksigning."

Fran used the material from her ezine in her book, but it's organized in the book more like an encyclopedia, whereas in the newsletter, items are spread out and jumbled. The newsletter has served her by allowing her to write the book, "Book Marketing from A to Z," to develop an expert site, to do some low-cost publicity for the subscribers and to start her radio program.

"My best subscribers are the one who are proactive, who send me marketing strategies, who pay their fees on time, and who are supportive."

She writes expert sheets for spirituality authors, along with a bio, and she sends them to the spirituality radio shows, some broadcast, some internet. She makes the connection and allows the hosts and journalists to follow up. She doesn't charge much, because she works by email, she doesn't do the follow up work or send press kits the way high paid publicist do.

Her biggest beef with the publishing industry is "the prejudice against POD and self-published authors. It's criminal that you can't get these books reviewed by the mainstream media. There is a tremendous amount of talent out there...but it takes so long to go the traditional route, a couple of my older writers told me it just takes too long because they didn't know for sure how long they were going to be around."

It is clear that newsletters are one way to networking with others who can bring sales to your book through the success-minded input of their marketing techniques, all tried and true.

📖 Internet Hazards and Ways to Waste Your Money

Pay-per click advertising: the deep well for advertising dollars.

Many publishers and authors use the pay-per-click PPC advertising as part of the marketing plan for their services and books. Sponsored links with Google, Yahoo and other major search engines are supposed to put an end to worries about whether or not your website will show up on the first or second page of the search engine's listings.

Nightengale Press used both Google and Yahoo PPC advertising for nearly a year, until the costs to compete with high volume and high-paying, larger publishers became unreasonably inflated. We were paying 5 cents per click and getting lots of click-through action in 2004, and by 2005 to compete we would have needed to pay over $2.50 per click. The volume of traffic dropped as our ability to pay higher and higher PPC rates diminished. So, we quit using PPC altogether and built a much more reliable affiliate program for our authors and our publishing business. Our affiliates are compensated only for sales from their sites, not from clicks on their sites, so we avoid this issue entirely.

But, here are some cautions from author, Linda Carlson's May 2006 PMA Independent article, *Click Fraud Alert: What you risk with Pay-per-Click*, for those of you considering or still using PPC.

"The two most prevalent types of click fraud are competitive sabotage, which can quickly drive your PPC ad costs up to a level you can't tolerate, and affiliate spam, which involves site owners clicking on ads that appear on their own sites to boost their share of ad

revenue from search engines such as Google or Yahoo.

"*Competitive sabotage* may be used by malicious competitors, unhappy customers, disgruntled employees, and others who want to hurt a PPC advertiser financially.

"*Affiliate spam* occurs on sites that carry sponsored links from a search engine and are compensated by a search engine, which splits its revenue for each click-through with the hosting site. Many thoroughly respectable companies include sponsored links on their sites, and there's no reason to suspect that they're inflating the number of clicks. But some Web sites apparently exist primarily to generate click-through revenue, and they attract advertisers by claiming high click-through rates, which they may create themselves."

Whether Nightengale Press's negative experience with PPC and the diminishing returns of this means of advertising was due to sabotage or affiliate spam is of no concern to me in sharing this information with readers. I have found that paying for advertising on the web is doubtful at best, perhaps even fool-hardy for those on limited advertising budgets. We have found that by networking and keeping connected, we draw better business to our site than when we advertised with PPC.

Most casual individual users and many small business users on the Internet are essentially unaware of how fast the climate is changing from a free-for-all concept to a pay-for-everything system that could seriously reduce the individual's and small business's ability to play on a level playing field. While many are not entirely happy with the "Amazon" way of doing business on the web, one thing has certainly occurred: the large business and the small business meet their customers in essentially the same fashion and playing by the same rules.

In the book business, this has revolutionized everything from printing to sales to fulfillment. But the halcyon days of the internet are threatened by those who would seek to end the concept of "free" in the free marketplace of the worldwide web.

Reid Goldsborough, a syndicated columnist and author of the book Straight Talk About the Information Superhighway explains in clear terms how fragile is the free internet as we know it today. He clarifies three potential hazards to the no-cost character of the internet in his July 2006 article in PMA Independent, *The End of the Free Internet? Pay-to-Send Schemes, Packet Prioritization and Taxing Internet Sales.*

"A key reason the Internet has succeeded as it has is that it's largely free, aside from the costs of getting onto it. But its success has been accompanied by more and more efforts to capitalize on it, from both private enterprise and the government. More changes loom ahead." The following are excerpts from his article in the PMA Independent.

Pay-to-Send Schemes

"One of the biggest online players, America Online, recently made the controversial move of giving preferential treatment to large emailers if they pay a fee to bypass its spam filters through Goodmail Systems' CertifiedEmail service (www.goodmailsystems.com).

"AOL's move will increase junk email...creating an unfair two-tier email system, with large companies able to pay to bypass AOL's malfunctioning spam filters, while small businesses, nonprofit organizations, and individuals are unable to reach many intended recipients... [that] everybody will eventually have to pay to be assured of fast and reliable email. In response, hundreds of small businesses and nonprofit organizations have teamed together to create the DearAOL. com Coalition (www.dearaol.com), applying pressure on AOL, Yahoo, and other Internet service providers to stop or reject such pay-to-send schemes. Among the members of the coalition are the liberal MoveOn.org and the conservative RightMarch. com political action committees. ...Pay-to-send email isn't a new concept; Microsoft talked about it a decade ago. But it has finally arrived.

Packet Prioritization

"...Telecommunications and cable companies have proposed schemes to offer preferential treatment to Web sites for the transmission of their data packets, for a fee. This 'packet prioritization' would enable those sites to be faster and more responsive than other sites....[Packet Prioritization] will also give large companies an unfair advantage and hurt small businesses, nonprofits, and individuals. Consumer groups and Internet companies such as Google and Amazon.com oppose packet prioritization...these organizations are lobbying [Congress] for 'Net neutrality,' also called 'network neutrality...' Individuals can [let] their elected representatives know how they feel. Faxes are more effective than email, and old-fashioned mailed letters are more effective than faxes. FreePress (www.freepress.net) is a group that lobbies for 'more democratic media.'

📖 Taxing Internet Sales

"Other Internet revenue–generating initiatives involve state governments seeking to increase their sales-tax revenues... to force residents to pay a "use tax" on merchandise bought over the Internet. More than 40 states are participating in the Streamlined Sales Tax Project (www.streamlinedsalestax.org), which is attempting to simplify state sales and uses tax codes to make the collection of sales and use taxes mandatory for out-of-state sellers. It receives funding from the National Governors Association and other organizations. NetChoice (www.netchoice.org) is a coalition of e-commerce companies such as Yahoo and eBay that opposes Internet use and sales taxes. Avalara (www.avalara.com) is a company seeking to benefit from them by offering to e-commerce sites software that calculates the sales tax customers owe on Internet purchases."

For more information about the free internet, contact Mr. Goldsborough at  www.reidgold@netaxs.com.

📖 📖 📖

The Internet seems to be an infinite place akin to the universe in size, and growing larger every second. While most cannot even wrap the mind around the concept of infinite, within one's own sphere of influence, it is possible to reach out further than ever before to grow a business, to sell a product, to make a name for oneself, to promote an idea, to sway public opinion and to create an identity or a brand that millions of others can reach. The time required and the hard work involved are no deterrent for those determined to access the potential for great rewards available on the Internet.

One of the larger mysteries of the Web is how to gain ranking for your website. One of the best explanations I have ever found was in Hope O. Kiah's Hope Kiah owns www.santafe-webdesign.com and was listed as one of the top 25 web design firms in New Mexico by the New Mexico Business Journal in 2002. Her site includes a Keyword Coach blog with free video tutorials. She also runs a southwest author promotion site, www.readsouthwest.com.

Search Engine Optimization (SEO) can be thought of as a set of techniques that enhance a web site's search engine ranking in response to specific search phrases. These techniques are always changing, and are well known to large firms with serious online competition. Freelancers, creatives, writers and small business owners are less likely to understand SEO. The irony here is that these smaller businesses can benefit much more easily from just a little attention to SEO. This is true for a couple of reasons:

The competition for a freelancer is likely to be another freelancer, who is just as unlikely to utilize web marketing. So a few steps can make the difference between no ranking and a high ranking in Google.

Web designers who build sites for small businesses are frequently unschooled and perhaps not interested in SEO. I was one of these designers, who focused on the look-and-feel of a site and didn't pay much attention to driving quality traffic to it. Since learning the ins and outs of keywords, I have been building sites with SEO in mind, working closely with the customer to build their traffic and web ranking.

My intent here is to outline some steps that you, as a site owner, can take to save hundreds or even thousands of dollars you might otherwise pay an SEO professional. This article outlines the basics. For a step-by-step tutorial, please visit www.santafe-webdesign.com and click on the Keyword Tutorial link. This PDF book will give you everything you need, including printable planning sheets, to organize your new or revised site in a way that can attract the quality and quantity of visitors that grow your business.

Key Steps for Web Marketing

Think about your market. Who are your existing customers? Describe them. Are your readers mostly women? What age? Make a list of attributes. Also think about your ideal reader. Who do you most want to attract? Make another list of attributes. The clearer you are about who you want to sell to, the more likely you are to find ways to attract them.

Imagine what both these groups type into search engines. Make a list of these phrases. Ask your existing readers what they would type if they were looking for your book! Ask your family. Ask your mother. It's really important to get away from your own imagination and find out what someone might truly type. These phrases are called keywords, even when they contain several words.

📖 **Get free help from Google.** Do a search in Google for: "google adwords keyword tool." The top result should take you to the Keyword Tool page where you can type a phrase into a field and get a table of results. Bookmark this page! You will use it many times.

📖 **Type your favorite keyword phrase into the text field and click on Get More Keywords.** A table will appear with four columns. The first column holds keyword phrases. You may see that Google has come up with a multitude of alternate phrases. This information is really important. The second column is the search volume for that phrase in the previous month. The volume is shown by a rectangular box with a green fill representing very low, low, average, high and very high volume. The third column represents Advertiser Competition, which is shown with the same graphic box. This column basically refers to how many web pages show up when you type that phrase into Google. The competition is web competition for that particular phrase.

📖 **Did your favorite phrase show up?** What is the search volume for that phrase? How is the competition? Start scanning down the table. Look for keywords that have a high search volume. Then look to the third column and see how much competition there is for those phrases. Start a spreadsheet of keywords, their search volume and their competition. (You're looking for search volumes that are higher than the competition.) Let these phrases inspire you! Maybe you wrote a novel about a Navajo detective. When you type "Navajo story" into the Google Adwords Keyword Tool, you may see that "Navajo book" is a much better keyword. You can "optimize" at least one page of your site for "Navajo Book" and help all those searchers find you!

📖 **Integrate the best keywords into your site.** Your web designer will be "optimizing" each page of your site for one to three keywords. If you found a really good phrase but you don't know where to put it, design a new page on your site that is devoted to that phrase. Give your web designer a text file for each page on your site with the keyword(s) at the top of the page. Say that you need the keyword in these places listed below. He or she will know what to do.

📖 **The title tag.** Give your designer a phrase that includes the keyword, with no more than 60 characters. Less is more, so don't feel you have to overdo it. Your Navajo Book page might have the title: John Taylor's latest Navajo Book.

📖 **The descriptive metatag.** Supply a short paragraph that will explain what this page offers in a way that uses the keyword and entices visitors to come to the page. Use up to 150 characters including spaces. When someone is looking at the results in Google, if your page comes up, they will see the title tag text as a link, and the descriptive metatag text below.

📖 **The keyword metatag.** Simply supply the keywords here, separated by commas

📖 **The H1 tag.** This shows up as the main header on the page. You can use just the keyword or embellish it slightly.

📖 **Bold or italic text.** Repeat the keyword up to 4 times in the body of your text with bold and/or italic text.

📖 **Linked text.** If you can use your keyword as a link, that's great! Search engines pay special attention to phrases that have a high search volume and show up on relevant web pages as links. It's especially good if you can put the link at the bottom of your web page. You might say at the bottom "More about John Taylor's latest Navajo Book," linking to a page about the book. And/or, you might use the text in the navigation on your site: HOME | ABOUT JOHN TAYLOR | NAVAJO BOOK | CONTACT. If the links are all text, not graphic buttons, then search engines can easily follow the links through your site.

📖 **ALT tags.** When supplying an image to your web designer, include a phrase that they can add to the code for the image, including a keyword if possible. These tags are intended for accessibility. If a sight-impaired person is visiting your site, they may have the text read to them by software. If so, the software will read the ALT tags and give them an idea of what the image is about. Be sure to give a simple description, but use keywords too if you can. Search engines pay attention.

📖 Links and Other Tips

Search engines like it when people link to you. Check on who is linking to your site by going to Yahoo and typing "linkdomain:www.yourdomain.com." Grow that list of linkers, so that the search engines will raise your ranking. Here are some ideas:

📖 **Article Directories** are sites that accept articles and post them for the public to use, with the understanding that any reprinting of the article will include credit for the author and a link to their site. Go to www.sitepronews.com/article-directories.html to find a list of article directories. I like goarticles.com, but you might find a directory that relates specifically to your subject.

📖 **Submit articles to these directories**, with links to your site included in the signature. Sprinkle keywords tastefully through the text. If possible, use the keyword itself as the link back to your site in your signature. You will benefit most from this if you first post the article on your own site. You may want to create an ARTICLES section of your site to grow your content. Search engines LOVE relevant content possibly more than any other SEO technique. If you post the article to your site first, then your site will get the most credit for the content. You will still get the value of "back links" from other sites that post your article, but your site will get the most ranking value for the article.

📖 **Ask for relevant links.** Are you member of a writer's association? Will they link to you? Do you have readers who like your books? Do they have websites? Ask them to link to you. Is your book a how-to book that relates to art? Maybe there is an art shop that will link to you from their site, or sell your book! Get creative.

📖 **Avoid link building schemes.** There are many companies that will try to sell you services that will create links to and from your site to other sites. Don't bother. The kind of links you want are from relevant sites. A thousand junk links from unrelated sites are pretty useless.

📖 **Blog Blog Blog!** Google now owns Blogger which is a free service for creating a blog. Go to Blogger.com and click the Take a Quick Tour button. Also look at the help menu. It's easy! A blog is a simple way to grow relevant content that search engines will track. And it's fun! You don't need to know any coding to do it. The important thing is to use keywords every so often when you make a post. Highlight the keyword in the post and click on the LINK tool icon. A dialogue box will open up with a field for the link. Paste the address to your website, or even better, to a specific page on your site that is optimized for the keyword you have highlighted. This is a powerful way to impress Google, but it can backfire on you if you use it too much. The best way to avoid getting red-flagged is to make sure your blog is hosted on your server with your website. Your web designer can help you with this.

📖 **Keep the site current.** Out of date web pages are horrible for your image.

📖 **Help your visitors know what to do!** The web can be a baffling experience. Visitors to your site will not mind being given instructions. Help them out by using action verbs and make suggestions like "Sign up for our Newsletter," "Buy Now," "Read Our Articles," "Visit our Blog" and "Call Us." These suggestions are "Calls to Action." Make them visible and repeat them on every page of your site if possible.

For a comprehensive set of steps, go to www.santafe-webdesign.com and click on Keyword Tutorial.

📖 Make the most of Internet Talk Radio and Pod-Casts to boost sales

Internet talk radio is a growing entity, which provides low-cost high-value opportunities for anyone who needs to promote themselves, a product or a business. Giving interviews helps to establish you as an expert in your area of interest. Authors and people in the book industry are wise to participate as often as possible.

The main difference between a internet radio program and a podcast is that the internet radio program airs live at a specified time each week and then is archived for future listening. A podcast is first recorded and then made available to iPod downloadable devices. A podcast is never a live show on air.

Typically, the internet radio show host and the guests call into a conference call service. Then, the program is aired live with mucic bumpers, commercials and the occasional odd moment when the guest forgets to call-in. On a podcast, the host calls the guest and then the show is recorded for later download.

As an internet radio talk show host, I have the opportunity to interview authors and business people who work in the publishing industry every week on CALLING ALL AUTHORS. My station is Global Talk Radio, a fast growing internet station in Los Angeles. Go to www.globaltalkradio.com/shows/callingallauthors to listen to the archives of my program and to learn more about the station itself. This is not a free service. The monthly rate is $415 for full service, and other internet stations ask similar fees, some more, some less, but I can say I am completely happy with the excellent support and service at Global Talk Radio.

Authors and publishing industry experts appear with me on the show each week, and for each program, we have a routine that works well for us and for our guests. Here are some tips and details of etiquette that apply to any interview with the media, including newspapers, television interviews and radio interviews.

- **Be prepared.** Provide your host with six to ten talking points you'd like to discuss at least a week before the interview. Organize these points in a logical order and actually use them when you are on the air.
- **Keep the appointment and be on time.** There is nothing more impolite than to not show up, or to show up late for an interview. Unless you've had a serious calamity in your life, call in at the appointed time. Make it a priority to participate. If you can't make the interview, call or email the host at least day ahead. Please, do not just "not show up." You will not be invited back—ever.
- **Speak clearly.** Remember that you are talking to promote yourself, your book or your business. Slow down if you usually talk too fast, speed up if you usually talk too slowly, and speak loudly enough to be heard. It is amazing how often people mumble into the phone. And, don't breathe heavily into the phone, the air muffles the conversation.
- **No multi-tasking.** Turn off your computer, or turn away from it so you are not tempted to multi-task. Close the door to the room and ask your family to stay away till you come out after your interview. Please, don't do the dishes or tidy up your office while you are talking.
- **Be polite and cheerful.** Smile! It is okay to be happy on the program. Even if your topic is serious, an occasional, appropriately light-hearted comment is a good thing.

Remember, you are showing who you are, so a cheerful demeanor goes a long way help listeners hear what you are saying.

- **Give the host a chance to interact with you.** Be complete in your answers to all questions, but don't run on for several minutes without pausing. The host may have a question your listeners are thinking too, and if he/she can ask the question, your interview is even more valuable to you.
- **Use an outline for your responses.** All too often guests read from a written text. At the most, have your talking points list and a few short comments for each so you remember what you want to say about each item. But, do not write out a long answer. The temptation is to read it, as this kills the conversational style of an interview.
- **Be sure to give your website URL.** Your host will ask you to say what your website or email address is so listeners can contact you. Work it out ahead of time how to most easily give this information. Most people know you need the www. Ahead of the website, so you don't really have to say that part anymore. Point out anything unusual about the address—perhaps a number or a strange spelling is part of your URL. Make sure to clarify that as you give the information.

- **After the interview is over, write a quick thank you email to your host.** This goes a long way to getting yourself invited back on the show. Keep in touch with the show host for future events you'd like to publicize. Being on talk shows is a very valuable form of exposure, and the more of them you can do, the better.

CALLING ALL AUTHORS—Valerie Connelly

📖 And, if there is a way to advertise on the show's home page, for a reasonable cost, jump in. There are plenty of other people who come to the show's archives, and will see your display ad. It may encourage them to listen to your interview as well, and if you are running a commercial, everyone who hears it will connect with you long after your show airs.

An excellent new resource for finding radios shows to approach is Francine Silverman's new book called TALK RADIO FOR AUTHORS, Getting interviews Across the U.S. and Canada. ($17.95, ISBN 0-7414-3787-2 Infinity Publishing 2007)

Conclusion

As I put the finishing touches on this book, I realize how lucky I am to have walked this road, not only for myself, but for the authors we serve at Nightengale Press. I have a constant flow of new authors who come to our press by word of mouth. That is the greatest compliment the writing world can pay to a publisher. When my authors recommend Nightengale Press to someone, I feel humbled by the confidence they have in our work. When other writers, or publicists, marketing gurus, or even other publishers recommend our press to writers looking for a safe haven in this crazy world of making books, I am delighted and honored that we have made our press a welcome place for those looking to put their hearts into words for all to read.

Publishing books requires a good head for business, a clear sense of purpose, a willingness to take risks based on an educated guess, and a desire to make the best effort for the author. There are plenty of people in this business, as in any business, out for themselves first.

Once upon a time, someone asked me how it felt to be a new publisher. I replied, "It's a bit like being a goldfish swimming with sharks." But I have also found there are wonderful people who are publishers, printers, distributors, suppliers and marketing wizards. I am reminded everyday, it takes all kinds of people to make the world. To me, writers are the best people on earth. Most are caring, giving and intelligent. What more could you ask every day than to be working with and for that kind of group? Thank you all for coming with me on this adventure. I hope this book helps you find your way.

CONTRIBUTORS

Authors of PMA Independent Articles quoted in the Publisher's Corner on the Calling All Authors Radio Show

Linda Carlson — infor@lindacarlson.com
Dave Cole — dcole@baytreepublish.com
Diane K. Danielson — info@downtownwomensclub.com
Kathi Dunn — www.dunn-design.com
Reid Goldsborough — reidgold@netaxs.com
Eric Gruber — eric@articlemarketingexpert.com
Brian Jud — brianjud@bookmarketingworks.com
Susan Kendrick — info@writetoyourmarket.com
Hope O. Kiah — www.santafe-webdesign.com
Florrie B. Kichler — fkichler@patriapress.com
Jan Nathan — jan@pma-online.com
Melanie Rigney — info@editorforyou.com
Bob Seidensticker — bob@future-hype.com
Ken Sturgis — gksturgis@earthlink.com
Lee Wilson — Lwilson@allworth.com

Guests Quoted from Interviews on the Calling All Authors Radio Show

Peter Chamlis, Marketing, ForeWord Magazine
pete@forewordmagazine.com

Shirley Cheng, Author shirley@shirleycheng.com

Pat DiPrima, Writing Coach ACE192@CLCILLINOIS.EDU

Lee German, Publisher, Sylvan Dell Publishing
LeeGerman@SylvanDellPublishing.com

Zara Griswold, Author surrogacybook@comcast.net

Bob Gussin, Publisher, Oceanview Publishing BobG@BOBGUSSIN.COM

John Henderson, Author jrh828@webtv.net

Carolyn Howard-Johnson, Author hojonews@aol.com

Colleen Kappeler, Editor info@wisconsinwriters.com

Kathleen Kearny, Editor KOBYKATHLEEN@MSN.COM

Chuck McCann, Author chuckmccann@npauthors.com

Maryglenn McCombs, Publicist maryglenn@maryglenn.com

Alex Moore, Managing Editor alex@forewordmagazine.com

Yvonne Perry, Writing Coach write_on_yvonne@comcast.net

Francine Silverman, Author, Newsletters franalive@optonline.net

Michael Stadther, Author www.alchemistsdar.com

Barbara Theesfeld, Author (contact information not available)

Patrika Vaughn, Editor, Publisher AdvoHouse@aol.com

John Washburn, Author whenevilprospers@yahoo.com

Irene Watson, Reviewer admin@readerviews.com

Alison Wilmes, Librarian awilmes@grayslake.lib.il.us

📖 INDEX by Chapter

Chapter 1: Who is Your Reader?   19
Bestsellers, Past and Present, 21
Bestseller Chart, 22
    Important Idea, 23
    Reader Identification, 23-24
    Person looking for the book, 25-26
    Author's life, 26-27
    Why recommend the book, 28-29
Your Answers to the five questions, 31-32
Notes, 33

Chapter 2: Genre—Who are you as an author?   34
Authors:
    Barbara Theesfeld, 35
    John Henderson, 36-38
    John Washburn, 38-41
    Zara Griswold, 41-42
    Michael Stadther, 42-44

Chapter 3: Where will you find your audience?   46
Bull's Eye Approach, 50-51
    Buzz, 52-53
    Maryglenn's Eight Points, 54
    Children's Books, 55
    Associations, 55-57
    Book Clubs, 57-58
    Museums, 58-59
    Schools, 59-60
Bull's Eye Zone Planning, 62-67
Success is hard work, 68

Chapter 4: Why you must write, edit, re-write, and re-edit. 69

It isn't enough to write a book, 69-74
    So you want to be a writer? 70
    It is really not that simple, 71
    Writing is a job, 71
    Commit to a time, 72
    Research everything, 72
    To outline or not to outline, 72-73
    Professional editor and proofreader, 73
    Learn from others, 73-74
    Writing Coaches, 74-75
    Continuing Education, 75-77
        Training, 76
        Skills, 77
        Books and Magazines, 78
        Correspondence & Online Courses, 78-79
        Community Colleges & Universities, 79
        Shaw Guides, 79-80
        Writing Groups, 80-81
    Editors, 82-84
        Developmental editing, 82
        Point of view editing, 82
        Grammar and Syntax, 82-83
        What editing is NOT, 83
        Pricing, 83-84
    Punctuation and Grammar, 84—89
        Paragraph spacing and format, 85
        Commas, etc., 85-86
        Ellipsis and Em Dashes, 86
        Italics, 86-87
        Computer Spelling/Grammar Functions, 87-88
        Online Resources 88-89
        Getting the details right, Quiz 89-92

Chapter 5: Can you tell a book by its cover? 93

Covers, 94-95
Titles, 95-97
No right or Wrong to Cover Design, 97
Internet Viewing, 98
Non-fiction, 98
Historical Fiction, 99
Horror, 99
Thriller, 100
Children's, 101
The Spine, 102-105
Review, 106

Chapter 6: How hard is it to sell a book? 107

Authors are true believers, 107
Shirley Cheng, 108
Chuck, McCann, 108
Michael Stadther, 108-109
The Three P's and I Don't Mean Vegetables, 109
    Planning, 110-111
        Creation Planning, 110
        Marketing Planning, 111
    Practice, 112
    Persistence, 112-114
Bookstores, Libraries, and Alternative Markets, 114-118
    Bookstores, 114
    Libraries, 114
    Amazon Bestseller List ,115-118
The Frugal Book Promoter, 118-120
Planning Checklists, 121-123

Chapter 7: How will you market your book?

The Marketing Plan, 124-126
The Public Relations Food Chain, 127-128
The PR Pyramid, 128-134
Reality, 134-136
Media, 136
    Newspaper Articles, 137
    Radio Interviews, 138
    TV Interviews, 138
    Market Definition, 139-140
    Website, 140
    Author Events, 140-143
Targeted Co-op Advertising, 143-144
Tradeshows, 144-145
Reviews, 145-153
Review Services, 153-158
    For Fee, 153-156
    For Free, 156-158
Awards, 158-161
    Book of the Year, 159
    Benjamin Franklin, 160
    IPPY, 160
    Parent to Parent, 160-161
Publicity Timelines, 162-182
    First publicity Timeline, 163-170
    Second publicity Timeline, 171-182
Your Website, 183
Your Blog, 184
Notes, 184

Chapter 8: Printing—Since the Gutenburg Bible   185
    Evolution, 185-188
    Lightning Source, 189
    Battle Royal, 190
    Online Bookstores, 190
    Risks, 190
    Warehousing is a thing of the past, 191
    Downside to digital printing, 191
        Pricing, 191-192
    Offset Printing Quotes, 192
    Wholesalers vs. Distributors, 192-193.
    Publisher Website Pricing, 193-194
    Experience is the best teacher, 194-195

Chapter 9: The Publishing Revolution—Knowledge is Power   196
    Self-Publishing, 197-199
    Nightengale Press, 200-204
    Large Self-Publishing Vanity Presses, 205-208
    Commercial Publishers, 208-210
    Publishing Misconceptions, 211-212
    Misconception-busting Questions, 212-216
    Checklist, 217

Chapter 10: Reality Breaks the Mold—Setting Realistic Expectations   218
    What is Success? 219
    What about getting an agent? 220-224
    More about Fee-based Publishers, 224-225
    More Common Unrealistic Expectations, 226-230
    Review What You Have Learned, 231-234

Chapter 11: Press Releases & Better Press Coverage — 235
    Brian Jud's Press Release Guide, 236-244
    Prfree.com, 244
    Prweb.com, 244-245
    Getting Better Press Coverage, 246-250
    Practice Makes Perfect, 252
        Press Release Exercise, 253-259
        Notes, 260

Chapter 12: The Essentials of the Internet — 261
    Writing a Book is a business, 261-264
    The website: Essential as Breathing, 264
        You absolutely must have a website, 264-265
    Ezines, E-newsletter and Blogs, 265-273
        Blogging Tips and Tricks, 266
        Linkers and thinkers, 267
        How to begin a blog, 267
        Elements of a good blog, 267-269
        Simple steps, 270
        Ezines, use articles to boost book sales, 270-271
            Step 1: Target your audience, 271
            Step 2: Grab your readers, 271-272
            Step 3: Turn readers into prospects, 272
            Step 4: Make a squeeze page, 272
            Step 5: Submit article, build links and traffic, 272-273
        Newsletters, 273-275
        Internet Hazards & Waste Money, 275-279
            Pay-per-click advertising, 275-276
            Pay-to-send schemes, 277-279
        Boost Search Engine Ranking, 280-286
    Internet Talk Radio and Podcasts, 287-290
    Conclusion, 291

Contributors — 293
Rate Yourself Quiz Answers — 301
About the Author — 303

📖 RATE YOURSELF QUIZ ANSWERS from Page 91-92

___I know the difference between prepositions and interrogatives. Some common prepositions are:
IN, AT, ON, OVER, UNDER, BEHIND, IN FRONT OF, THROUGH, WITH, TO, BESIDE, NEXT TO, AFTER, BEFORE, INSIDE, OUTSIDE, ABOVE, BELOW

The interrogatives are: WHO, WHAT, WHERE, WHEN, HOW

___I know adverbs modify verbs. He drove FAST on the expressway.

___I know adjectives modify nouns. The BIG dog ate the SMALL bone.

___I know subject pronouns are:
I, YOU, HE, SHE, IT, WE, YOU, THEY

___I know the possessive pronouns are:
MY, YOUR, HIS, HER, ITS, OUR, YOUR, THEIR

___I know what the pluperfect tense is. Example sentence:
I HAD KNOWN all along that the cat HAD BEEN TRAPPED on the roof during the flood.

___I know how to use the conditional tense accurately with other tenses. Examples sentence:
If I HAD enough money, I WOULD BUY a new car.

___I know what the Past Conditional Tense is. Example sentence:
If I HAD KNWON his name, I WOULD HAVE CALLED OUT to him.

___ I know there are two kinds of present tense. They are the SIMPLE PRESENT and the PRESENT PROGRESSIVE
I LIVE in a small town.   I AM LIVING in a small town.

___ I know there are two kinds of past tense. They are the SIMPLE PAST and the PAST PROGRESSIVE
I LIVED in a small town.   I WAS LIVING in a small town.

___ I know how to use the future tense. Example sentence:
Next year, I WILL GO to France on vacation.

___ I know what the future anterior tense is and when to use it. Example sentence:
By this time next year, I WILL HAVE GONE to France on vacation.

___ I know what the passive voice is: Example sentence:
The dog was fed too much food by the little boy.

___ I know what the active voice is: Example sentence:
The little boy fed the dog too much food.

___ I know the articles. They are: A, AN and THE

___ I know what the demostrative articles are:
THIS, THAT, THESE THOSE

___ I know what a gerund is. Example sentence:
Reaching for the dollar in his pocket, Jack bought a candy bar for his sister.

There is much more to knowing grammar and using it well than I can present here, but if you pass this test, you have a fair grasp of some of the basics.

Passing means getting ALL these answers right without looking anything up.

Born, raised and a resident in Illinois for most of her life, Valerie Connelly now lives with her husband, Michael, in Wisconsin north of Milwaukee. She divides her time between publishing, writing, speaking, painting landscapes and waterscapes, and traveling.

An educator and international traveller since her days as a Peace Corps volunteer in Togo, West Africa in 1969, Valerie Connelly taught French language and literature in Illinois from 1974-2005. She holds a MA in French Literature from Northwestern University. In the 1980's she founded the nonprofit organization, Overseas Alliance, to travel with her students in France to study art, history and architecture, live in French families, and to meet with her most famous friend, then French President François Mitterrand. Every year for five years, M. Mitterrand invited Ms. Connelly and her students to the Elysée Palace for the diplomatic celebrations after the parade down the Champs Elysée on July 14th.

Ms. Connelly has also traveled and worked in other parts of the world. In addition to teaching for two years in West Africa, she wrote the English Language curriculum and helped set up a school in Iran in 1973, prior to the fall of the Shah. She has traveled extensively in Europe. And between teaching responsibilities, she researched and wrote about far-flung parts of the world as a copywriter for a major wholesale luxury tour operator.

Ms. Connelly founded Nightengale Press in July of 2003. By January of 2007 Nightengale Press has published more than fifty books with several more coming into print every month. Nightengale Press is now part of Nightengale Media LLC offering its authors a first class website, bookstore, marketing opportunites and more.

Ms. Connelly is also an internet radio talk show host on GLOBAL TALK RADIO, and you can listen to the show archives at www.globaltalkradio.com/shows/callingallauthors.

Go to www.www.nightengalepress.com for complete publishing information. JOIN www.callingallauthors.org to learn and share.

📖 IN THE BEGINNING I WAS A SINGER/SONGWRITER...

📖 Singing in 1967

📖 Concert in 1969

📖 Modeling Saks Fifth Avenue 1968

📖 Singing in 1992

📖 FOR A LONG WHILE I WAS A TEACHER 1969-2005...

📖 C.C.O. De Tabligbo, Togo, West Africa
Peace Corps Volunteer Educator 1969-1971

📖 With French President François Mitterrand and Students 1985

📖 4TH YEAR HONORS FRENCH Students 2004   📖 Phi Delta Kappa
                                              TEACHER OF THE YEAR 2005

📖 BLOCKART PRINTS EVOLVED INTO NIGHTENGALE PRESS...

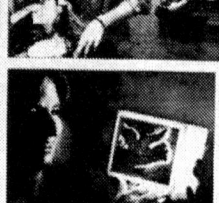

A chip off the old block

Artist uses (slight) update in technology to print more cards

📖 Print Shop for Custom Greeting Cards & Patented Glowbox

📖 Publisher at Work

📖 NOW I AM A PUBLISHER / AUTHOR / TALK SHOW HOST
2003–the Present...

📖 Signing at Borders, Gurnee IL 2003

📖 Signing In booth at BookExpo America, Chicago 2004

📖 Signing at BookExpo America, NYC 2005

📖 MORE TITLES BY VALERIE CONNELLY

SACRED NIGHT $13.95
ISBN 09743348-0-4

This mystery-thriller with a layer of fantasy that takes the reader from the streets of Chicago to the jungles of the Amazon and back, as Detective James Cameron embarks on the most challenging investigation of his career to unravel the mystery of SACRED NIGHT.

SIDETRACKS $14.95
ISBN 09743348-2-0

A mystery-thriller with a touch of fantasy and a bit of romance. This book explores treachery and deceit from the corporate boardroom to the most dangerous and deadly rivalry of all: one's own family.

ARTHUR, THE CHRISTMAS ELF $24.95 Full Color
ISBN 1-933449-23-3

A story book that will keep on giving long after the read-aloud part is done. This tale about two self-absorbed children, a storm and Santa's elf, Arthur, will help kids gain a new perspective on Christmas gifts in both the giving and getting departments.

The author-illustrated 43-page story is only the first part of this two-part book. In the second part are instructions on how to make the craft projects mentioned in the story. These easy-to-make, family-tested projects provide instructions are well-organized, easy to follow and include traceable patterns and photographs that illustrate the projects step by step.

Order at
www.nightengalepress.com
And www.arthurthechristmaself.com
And All online stores
Also available through
Ingram & Baker & Taylor

As a SPEAKER Valerie's Expertise Can Reach Your Audiences

MOST REQUESTED TOPICS:
CALLING ALL AUTHORS - HOW TO PUBLISH WITH YOUR EYES WIDE OPEN

Publishing: All Risk, No Security.
Valerie outlines the phenomenal growth of the publishing industry and how that growth affects every author's chance of finding success for his book. A no-nonsense look at reality in publishing.

Marketing: All Risk, No Security.
Valerie reveals Myths, Misconceptions and Realities about the author's responsibilities and the Publisher's responsibilities when it comes to marketing.

Writing: You'll Need More Than a Laptop to Write a Book
Valerie provides authors with valuable and useful information on writing and creating a salable book.

Believing in Yourself, Your Book and Your Passion
Valerie gives away the driving force that has guided her through every stage of her working life with humorous, poignant, anecdotal and real life experiences and how you can make these ideas work for you, too.

Valerie's CALLING ALL AUTHORS™ presentation brings all her talents as a speaker, singer, educator and talk show host together in a no-nonsense look at the publishing industry. Humor and music compliment the compelling, first-hand information and entertaining format she provides your writer's conference.

As an entertainer, Valerie's humor and musical talents personalize her message. As an educator, she delivers useful, no-nonsense information in a practical and accessible way. As a motivator, she will provide tangible and inspiring ways to apply the myth-busting content of her talk to every writer's life and writing career.

Valerie is a member of the National Speaker's Association, Wisconsin Chapter

WHAT CLIENTS ARE SAYING About Valerie's Presentations

Excellent presentation. Very well organized and informative. You have something one cannot learn — a sense of humor. Never lose that!
— Anthony Ramos, Barnes & Noble Writers Group

Great! Very entertaining & great speaker. I'll come back. Thanks for the fun!
—Prosenet Writers Group Attendee

I thoroughly enjoyed the presentation. It was informative and interesting --- a whole new line of information.
—Josh Barnes, Barnes & Noble Writers Group

Valerie provided an excellent overview of a new way to publish.
—Susan Remson

The best part was talking about the nuts and bolts of the publishing industry, your business and the Q&A.
— Ron Larson, Barnes & Noble Writers Group

Very interesting and I enjoyed the insight into the publishing business.
— Brian J. Barnes, Barnes & Noble Writers Group

Very enjoyable!
—Don Lumbee, Prosenet Writers Group

My expectations were exceeded. Valerie was very informative and her style was awesome!
—A New World: Publishing in the 21st Century Attendee

All great! Above and beyond!
—A New World: Publishing in the 21st Century Attendee

Go to www.wisconsinspeakers.com
To see videos and learn more about Valerie's Availability as a SPEAKER

📖 www.callingallauthors.org - TO LEARN THE BUSINESS OF AUTHORING A BOOK

It takes more purpose than just writing the book to make a book succeed. Be honest with yourself. Do you want to go to all that trouble, write, re-write, pay editors, find a publisher, put your book out there, only to have it languish in obscurity? Of course not. Why would you want to do that? Your status as a Member on www.callingallauthors.org will bring others toward you, your book, your expertise, and your website, too. How can that be? Well, because this is a place where YOU can shine, develop connections, highlight your events and books, share information, tips and tricks about writing, publishing and marketing of books, learn, teach, and exercise your networking skills.

You stand to benefit from these opportunities:
- 📖 to blog right on the site
- 📖 contribute articles right on the site
- 📖 release your news right on the site
- 📖 save on the educational products offered only on the site
- 📖 and grow from the experience as never before
- 📖 you can link to us and we will link to you
- 📖 you can agree to link to other members of complimentary mind or genre or expertise, or to others who are different and that will drive traffic in all directions
- 📖 your willingness to share will bring more to you than you can even imagine.

Every month there will be an entertaining informational teleseminar to attend, a downloadable informational video to learn from. Every other month there will be an entertaining Webinar with more reality-based information. Once every three months a new library of audio-clips will be released, and there will be downloadable PDFs to inspire, inform and motivate you. And as the site grows, the offerings will grow too. How do you Join? You will first need to Register to see what's available, and you need to be a Member to get all the bells and whistles. I invite you to join www.callingallauthors.org. You'll be glad you did!

📖 WHAT AUTHORS ARE SAYING About Nightengale Press

You take 'dreams' and graciously make them 'realities'. Your continual correspondence makes any author feel secure and well-taken care of. I am amazed at the diversity of your talents, Valerie...Your expertise and guidance are invaluable to us all...The personal touch you give, means the world to me, and other's I'm sure! Thanks and keep up the great job!

—Jodi Pliszka, M.S. Author/Illustrator

Ms. Valerie Connelly and her leadership has been an inspiration to me as a fledgling author...As writer I have experienced her professional diligence and the indefatigable work ethic...Her constant striving for perfection is, and will remain, a constant source of guidance and strength to me... I consider her expertise as colleague invaluable. I cherish her guidance as friend, both immeasurable and irreplaceable...
—Stephen Taylor, Author, Toronto CANADA

I wanted to personally thank you for the outstanding job you've done so far with my novel, <u>Net Loss</u>. You've guided me through a very challenging process with lots of advice and coaching, never failing to respond to my flurry of questions. I may have asked the same question dozen of times, and sometimes been slow responding to your inquiries, but you have shown the patience and persistence needed to bring an inexperienced author along. I was also impressed by the quality of the actual book. Hold it side by side versus a book published by one of the giants, and you can't tell the difference. That quality was critical to me in selecting you as my publisher, and the final product exceeded my expectations. From designing the cover, to marketing my novel at a national expo, to providing links to key distributors, you have done everything possible to make my book a success. Thank you for all of your hard work.

—Tim Hein, Author

www.ingramcontent.com/pod-product-compliance
Ingram Content Group UK Ltd.
Pitfield, Milton Keynes, MK11 3LW, UK
UKHW021314180426
11947UKWH00015B/1225